How to
Launch a
Freelance
Copywriting
Business

Creative Writing
for a Living

JULES HORNE

Want to earn a living from your writing?
This straight-talking, practical handbook
will get you up and running quickly.

method
writing

Texthouse, Riverside Mills, Dunsdalehaugh, Selkirk, TD7 5EF
www.texthouse.co.uk

How to Launch a Freelance Copywriting Business: Creative
Writing for a Living / Jules Horne. — 1st ed.

Cover design and typesetting: Victor Marcos
www.99designs.com/profiles/victormarcos/services

ISBN
978-0-9934354-5-4 (paperback)
978-0-9934354-4-7 (e-book)

Contents

PART IV   149

STARTER PROJECTS   159

Introduction

This book is perfect for you if you're a creative thinker and writer who wants to earn a good living from your words. I wrote it to help creative writing students, journalists, and other skilled writers who've considered copywriting, but don't know whether it's for them, or how to get started.

It's based on my own experience of starting a successful copywriting business from scratch, without help, advice, or books like this to guide me. In the middle of the Scottish countryside. With skylarks for company. And woefully slow broadband. If I can do it, you can.

This book will help you cut to the chase, and get going quickly.

Note that it assumes you can already *write*. It assumes you're a demon speller and grammar-wrangler. It assumes that one of the following is true:

- you have a creative writing or English degree or MFA, or
- you're a journalist looking for another income stream, or
- you've written as part of your professional life, or
- your writing has been published in other ways.

If this is you, read on.

Writing for business is a way for skilled writers to earn a good, dependable income. Someone writes all the websites, brochures, and marketing materials out there. Why not you?

In business, the people who write copy often aren't writers. They may be business owners, or an employee who got landed with the job. They probably don't love writing as you do. They're probably less than good at it. In truth, their writing may be letting their business down badly. This is where you come in, with your magic pen and professional writing skills.

Businesses large and small *need* writers. They need them to make a connection with customers, to get the message out about their products, to sell and to survive.

Find that work, and you can make a good living, with work that's home-based and flexible, and fits well with family and creative life.

This book explains how to set up your freelance writing business, including:

- how to find customers and get paid work
- how to approach businesses professionally and with confidence
- how to wrangle money as well as words
- how to set up your workflow for greater productivity.

You'll also find recommended resources on copywriting and the distinct requirements of writing for business.

About Me

I'm a working writer based in rural Scotland, where there aren't any jobs for writers! So like most of us, I have a portfolio career. Over the years, as well as running my own copywriting business, Texthouse, I've written Edinburgh Fringe First-winning plays, BBC radio drama, fiction, and song lyrics. I also teach on the Open University Creative Writing MA. My background is in languages (a German and French degree at Oxford University), followed by several years as a journalist with the BBC World Service and Swiss Radio International.

I've always wanted to write full-time, and eventually returned home to work freelance. I now balance creative and commercial work to earn an independent living.

Why I Wrote This Book

I wrote this book because it wasn't around when I started out. I'm an ex-journalist and published writer. It should have been easy to figure out how to earn a good living. It took me several years of trial and error.

Why? Because when I started out, books on writing and business were aimed at agencies, marketers and companies with marketing teams. Enterprise training courses were equally hopeless for my needs. They were aimed at larger businesses, and traditional sectors such as manufacturing. Not sole traders looking for specific creative industries advice.

So that's what's in this book. Key takeaways include:

How to adapt your writing skills for business.
Your writing skills are valuable in a business context, but you'll first need some sales and marketing tools and concepts to build on what you already know about the craft of writing.

How to get work.
Creative writing qualifications are unlikely to impress anyone in the business world. You need to reframe your skills for the business context, with evidence that resonates with business people.

How to approach businesses.

Not all businesses need writing services. How do you find those that do? How do you present yourself? How do you demonstrate your value to potential clients?

How to handle money.

Rates vary between companies and sectors. How do you work out what to charge? How do you prepare a quote? Project, day, or hourly basis?

How to market yourself.

You don't need extrovert salesmanship. You do need to show the value of your services. Where do you start? Do you need a leaflet, cards, website?

How To Use This Book

This book is laid out so that you can read it straight through, use it as a reference, or follow it as a course. I suggest you skim-read first, to get a sense of the territory, then dive into the sections closest to your situation.

Don't expect to take in everything at once. Make notes as you go, and read the book again in six months' time. You'll take new insights from your different vantage point.

Don't try to tackle three fronts at once: marketing, admin, and writing. Instead, do a little of each at a time, to keep progress manageable.

Where To Start

* If you're completely new to copywriting, and want to know whether you might enjoy it, go to **Is It For You?**

- If you're a journalist or creative writer and want to understand how your skills translate to copywriting, head to **Writing Skills Audit.**
- If you're in a hurry to get your copywriting business started, zoom to **Kit & Caboodle.**
- If you already do copywriting, and want ideas to streamline your process and be more productive, head to **Systems** and **Nuts & Bolts.**
- If you're ambitious to grow your income or expand, read the section on **Business Growth.**

If you find this helpful and want to share suggestions of your own, I'd love to hear from you! After all, copywriting is evolving all the time, and we're all in this together. You can email me at info@ method-writing.com.

Save Time & Money

I wasted a lot of time by not understanding the markets for freelance copywriting, and approaching the wrong kind of business. I also wasted a lot of money because I didn't know the value of my skills, and often charged too little.

This book will save you years of floundering, by including:

- my mistakes, so you don't make them
- processes to follow
- practical advice to suit different writing backgrounds and skills
- information on how copywriting is changing, and the impact of the internet.

Acknowledgements

Huge thanks go to the following contributors who have helped with research, editing and much-appreciated insights: Claire Wingfield, Michael Scott (editorial); Victor Marcos (design); Morgaine Merch Lleuad, Sherrie McCarthy, Val Andrews, Alexandra Amor, Sonja Cameron, Anna Johnstone, Daisy Eddy (research).

And Finally

This book is all about empowering writers to develop their own freelance business, and passing on some the resourceful and entrepreneurial skills needed to survive in this fast-changing world. I hope you find it as rewarding as it has been for me, both creatively and financially.

Very best wishes for your independent writing life!

Jules

US quotation style and Oxford commas are used in this book. For downloadable templates and resources, visit www.method-writing.com/

PART I

Creative Writing for Business

Freelance creative writers and journalists make a living in many different ways, including publication, workshops, readings, teaching, and editorial shifts. Freelancers on the creative writing path often support themselves with low-paid flexible work of other kinds.

Copywriting is another way to earn a living as a writer. I'm amazed more writers don't do this! By adapting writing and editing skills you already have, you can:

- earn more
- be your own boss
- meet inspiring people
- be challenged creatively
- help others to succeed
- connect with your community.

You can also control your own workload, work where you like, and choose your hours and clients. Maybe you can only work in the mornings, or need to put in time on your novel? Maybe you want to hot-desk at your local café, library or business hub, or work on the train or plane? This flexibility is one of the great advantages of copywriting.

Writing for business isn't some kind of panacea. You'll still need to work demanding and sometimes unsocial hours. But it's better paid than creative writing or journalism, and it's on your own terms. This independence alone is tremendously empowering.

What's more, you get to overcome one of the serious perils of the writing life: isolation. Because as a business writer, you're part of your...

Local Business Community

The people who run small businesses are fascinating. I've met an international chocolatier (best copywriting job ever!), an award-winning medicinal herbalist, catwalk knitwear designers, fibre optic lighting engineers. I've also worked for housing associations, timber frame home builders, charities, museums, galleries, a dive tourism company, and murder mystery game designers.

It's been amazing to see the variety of ideas and working lives going on in my community, often under the radar. For me, going behind the scenes and gaining privileged access to intriguing new worlds is a tremendous bonus of copywriting.

I've found people in the small business community to be creative, independent-minded, individualistic, and passionate about their dreams. They can also be stubborn, obsessive and risk-taking, and often don't fit naturally into office life. They need to be resilient and pick themselves up, time after time. They work their socks off in pursuit of a vision others may not understand.

A lot like writers, in fact. Except that small businesses often have the extra responsibility of employing other people, keeping them in work, sustaining other families and livelihoods.

Small businesses are a vital part of the social fabric, community survival and connection. Copywriting has put me in touch with that, and got me outside the bubble of writing. And I've met enough stories, characters and hidden worlds to keep me creatively inspired for years.

So if your writing background has planted misconceptions about the world of business, it's time for a rethink.

In the next section, you'll find out what copywriting is, whether it's a good fit for you, and how to approach it from different writing backgrounds.

Copywriting & You

What's A Copywriter?

A copywriter is someone who writes for businesses. Your job is to help a business to sell its products and services, by writing effective words that connect with its customers.

When it comes to "selling," you may be thinking of "hard sell" types of text such as advertising or direct mail marketing letters (the *Reader's Digest* kind). But these aren't the main diet for most jobbing business writers. I don't do that kind of writing myself.

Mostly, as a writer for small businesses, you'll be writing website content, case studies, white papers, newsletters. Short form writing may include product packaging and descriptions. Digital writing forms include SEO (search engine optimization) content, blogs, and social media. For more on this, see **Writing for the Web**.

Explaining what you do

Be warned: people you meet may be unfamiliar with the term "copywriter." They often think you're something to do with copyright – maybe a kind of patent lawyer. Or a journalist (from "copy editor," "copy desk"). Once, someone thought I repaired photocopiers.

This is an occupational hazard. If you're dealing with people outside the creative industries, be prepared to use different terminology. I sometimes call myself a "business writer" or "web/SEO content writer," depending on the context I'm in.

 A Little Etymology

"Copywriter" comes from the mediaeval Latin *copiare* (to transcribe) and *copia* (abundance). Think of mediaeval scribes writing copious pages of beautiful manuscripts.

"Copy" meaning "a newspaper item" appeared in the mid-1800s.

"Copywriter" in its modern context of advertising and marketing appeared in 1911. But the word still lives on in newsrooms, where a "copy desk" is staffed by a "copy editor" who licks "draft copy" into shape.

Confusingly, journalists write "copy," but don't call themselves "copywriters."

Who goes in for copywriting?

There's no definitive career route into copywriting, and it's an unregulated profession. People who write for business come from all walks of life: journalism, English degree, creative writing, sales, marketing, advertising, or a business specialism. A quick, unscientific straw poll of professional copywriters I know revealed an English graduate; theology graduate; PR with a background in the diplomatic service; former local government administrator; salesman; marketer; web designer with a local radio background.

Increasingly, you also find copywriters with a business, IT or technical background. Some marketers and web designers also offer copywriting as an add-on service to their core business.

Since copywriting is unregulated, anyone can offer copywriting services. This makes life easy for you. In theory, you can simply hang out your sign, and off you go. But look out for...

7

Pirates & buccaneers

Since anyone can set up in business as a copywriter, many non-writers are seduced into doing so, often at unsustainably low rates. This is a similar situation to those friends/nephews/neighbours who moonlight as web designers. Anyone can knock out a website in a couple of hours, right? But anyone wanting professional standards of design, security, build, longevity and impact for their business doesn't go to a neighbour for a freebie.

The tragedy is that clients often don't know the difference. They're often looking for a copywriter because they themselves aren't good with words, and so they can't judge what they're given. This means there are inevitably fraudulent and incompetent copywriters out there. More than once, I've been called in to do a makeover job on substandard work, often riddled with spelling and grammar mistakes, clichés, or factual errors.

Happily, the problems were caught in time by a switched-on designer. But beautiful, high-value products very nearly went out accompanied by poor-quality words for which the client had paid a fortune.

So my plea is: if you don't have excellent writing skills, don't be a copywriter. It's like trying to be a professional dancer with no sense of rhythm. Or a professional accountant who can't add up.

You'll also need a gift for putting yourself in customers' shoes, speaking their language, and forming a strong connection. And if you have shaky spelling or grammar, forget it. A print brochure or signage may cost thousands. If you get the details wrong, you could let down your clients very badly, and cost them sales and reputation.

It's a highly responsible job. You have been warned.

That said, if these responsibilities worry you, you may have exactly the right mindset for copywriting. You'll put in the necessary care and effort to get it right.

Do You Need Specialist Knowledge?

You do need some marketing basics, which are covered in this book. Otherwise, business writing is a broad church, rather like journalism. The job will depend on your specialisms, skills, preferences, and market. There are some specialist areas, such as technical writing. But it's unlikely you'd go there without some background in the relevant industry.

Most copywriters don't start out as specialists. Like journalists, they gather sector and product knowledge as they go along, through research and experience.

This is just as well! Businesses which need copywriting are often in manufacturing, trades, and services – areas typically less familiar to the arts graduates who make up the majority of writers. Industries more closely linked to the arts – publishing, galleries, media, education – are full of other highly literate arts graduates, who may see less need for copywriting services.

So be prepared to get involved in subject areas that aren't your own, and gradually carve out a niche. And in the meantime, mine your existing skills and work background for possible specialisms.

Maybe you have particular experience in retail, technology, or the third sector? Maybe you have a technology park on the doorstep? Maybe you're a journalist and prefer long form writing and interviews? Maybe you're a marketer, or have a specialist sales background?

All these backgrounds can provide a strong starting point, and be developed over time into a USP (unique selling point). I started off writing for anyone in my local area who asked. I eventually narrowed this down, and found clients who are a good fit for my strengths in tourism, textiles, food and drink, games, and technology.

The key to a rewarding business is to match skills and experience to the right opportunities. The more you're known in a given niche, the more word spreads, and the more you can charge. Even if you start wide, be prepared to specialize.

Is It for You?

What makes a good copywriter? Here's a round-up of some helpful personality traits:

Enthusiasm

Don't do it just for the money. People who aren't enthusiastic about a product or service don't make an authentic job of selling it. Your lacklustre writing can sink your client's business.

Responsibility

You need to turn around jobs quickly, efficiently and to deadline, maintain client confidentiality, and be on your client's side. In this arena, you're a business professional, not a creative artist. Business people won't appreciate writer's block or lack of inspiration.

Curiosity

Most writers are interested in how other people and worlds tick. Natural curiosity will help you absorb new information and research quickly.

 TV Debunk #1: *Mad Men*

Fantasy world: Glamour, sex, suits, cigarettes and hairspray.

Real world: At your desk, with occasional forays into cold stock rooms and Google Analytics.

Remember: *Mad Men* has as much in common with modern copywriting as *Outlander* with modern Scotland.

Listening

Not all clients are expressive or can articulate their needs well. Sometimes, they can only clarify what they want by talking it through with an outsider – which is often you. A good copywriter is a good listener who is client-focused and asks good questions.

Trust

Confidentiality and a professional manner are a given. Over time, you'll pick up useful business skills, trends and developments. Don't give away business secrets.

Resilience

Client relationships are give-and-take. If you encounter robust feedback and moving goalposts, don't take it personally or get defensive. Your job is to solve your client's problems, and get paid for it.

 TV Debunk #2: *Dragon's Den*

Fantasy world: World domination, evil geniuses, mad inventors, crushed dreams.

Real world: At your desk, helping ordinary people to survive.

Remember: Success and failure in *Dragon's Den* don't equate to success and failure in real life.

Respect

Respect business culture by turning up for meetings on time, and hitting deadlines. Your contribution may be part of a workflow leading to a website launch, or a trade show. Mission-critical!

Confidence

You don't need to be an extrovert. You do need to come across as confident in your skills. If you're shy, let your portfolio samples and testimonials speak for you.

Empathy

You need the imagination to put yourself in your client's shoes, and really understand and feel their enthusiasm for the product. Even more importantly, you need to empathize with the customers they want to reach.

Lack of ego
Copywriting isn't about you. Be aware that writing which draws attention to itself too much can sometimes get in the way of customer connection.

Phone skills
Most copywriters do a lot of their work on the phone, or via Skype. You may never meet the client in person. Skype use is particularly common among creative professionals such as web and graphic designers.

Tech skills
A touch of geekiness is an advantage in a culture where you'll work a lot with web-savvy designers and developers. Website (SEO) copywriting in particular calls for some technical understanding.

 TV Debunk #3: *The Apprentice*

Fantasy world: Epic blunders, ruthless bullies, and astonishing egos.

Real world: At your desk, helping your local chocolatier/ restaurant/kids' clothing start-up/housing association.

Remember: Your business community needs *you*. And would probably run a mile from these guys.

Writing Skills Audit

Fiction, journalism, poetry and scriptwriting are very different writing forms, and some of their associated skills translate more readily to copywriting than others. Here's an overview of some writer profiles, with typical strengths for copywriting, and potential skills gaps.

Creative writing graduate

As a creative writing graduate, you've mastered techniques such as voice, characterization, storytelling and viewpoint. You're also good at coming up with original ideas, and have strong grammar and editing skills.

Watch out for: wordiness, one of the dangers of great verbal fluency; self-consciously clever writing which draws attention to itself rather than the product or service. Try writing to a specific length or space, as journalists do.

Work on: concision, marketing, interviewing.

Fiction writer

As a fiction writer, you're a natural storyteller, and good at writing empathetically from different viewpoints. You're also good at long-form structure, and familiar with techniques such as hooks, reversals, plants and pay-offs.

Watch out for: wordiness – economical expression is crucial; invention, embellishment, and straying from the facts. Try using the marketer's *features and benefits* and the journalist's *who, when, where, why, what, how* to stay on track.

Work on: concision, marketing, interviewing.

Scriptwriter

If you've written for the screen, stage or radio, you're used to collaboration, ruthless feedback and editing, economical expression, and working to tough deadlines. You're also audience-aware, and good at writing spoken register.

Watch out for: spelling and grammar. These aren't such a concern in performed work, but need to be highly accurate in copywriting. Try the Grammarly website and see whether your editing standards pass muster.

Work on: proofreading, marketing, interviewing.

13

Poet

If you're a published poet, you excel at precision, economy, and attention to detail, and have a strong grasp of rhythm and metaphor. You're likely to be good at editing others, and collaborating with designers on visual layout.

Watch out for: heightened register and language, which can get in the way of customer connection; sensitivity to robust feedback. Practise shifting viewpoints and putting yourself in the client's and customers' shoes.

Work on: spoken register, marketing, interviewing.

Industry specialist

If you're an industry specialist, you'll have insider expertise, good contacts and awareness of trade magazines, sites and influencers. You may already have sales or marketing experience, and excel at B2B writing.

Watch out for: conflict of interest, business confidentiality; "inside the box" insider thinking; jargon. Be doubly vigilant about blurred lines, trade press contacts, and ethics.

Work on: creative writing techniques, customer viewpoint, journalism ethics.

Journalist

As a journalist, you're trained in a clear, lean writing style, and experienced in research, asking incisive questions, and spotting good story angles. You excel at cutting through complexity, and working to tight deadlines.

Watch out for: conflict of interest, especially if also doing PR, and mixing editorial with marketing work; too much authoritative "telling" vs more evocative, empathetic "showing."

Work on: showing, creative writing techniques, ethics.

IT specialist

As an IT specialist, you're likely to have good industry contacts and insider knowledge, as well as web and SEO skills. This makes you a good fit for B2B, technical writing, and possibly Analytics and digital marketing.

Watch out for: conflict of interest when dealing with industry clients; SEO-led writing, which can sound schematic and unengaging. Try using sensory detail to evoke vivid pictures, and verbatim quotes for authenticity.

Work on: marketing, creative writing techniques, storytelling.

Marketer

As a marketer, you're experienced in business and sales culture, and have a valuable strategic overview. You're skilled at pulling together creative teams, and may have digital marketing skills.

Watch out for: cliché and received ideas about written style; spelling and grammar issues. Try using sensory detail to evoke vivid pictures, and verbatim quotes for authenticity.

Work on: creative writing techniques, storytelling, viewpoint.

What's next?

Decide which kind of writing background is closest to yours. This will give you a clearer idea of your strengths, and where you fit into the copywriting ecology. In the meantime, work on your skills gaps. See **Resources** for recommended reading.

Copywriting in Context

As a typical arts graduate, I went into copywriting without business training, and learned business skills the hard way, through study, practice, trial and error.

It took me years to appreciate that business was a specific discipline with its own valuable concepts. It's useful to study these, as they apply not just to clients' businesses, but also to your own. The main ones are covered in **Business Concepts & Culture**. In the meantime, to set up a context for client businesses and your writing business, it's helpful to understand the...

Business Lifespan

Like people, businesses have a lifespan. They're born, grow, survive, and sometimes die. It's a useful metaphor, as it turns business from an amorphous blob to a set of clearly defined stages, with their own characteristics and challenges.

Knowing how other businesses have tackled these stages will help you to address them quicker. Identify what stage you're at, then use the suggestions in the rest of the book to get where you want to be. The five stages are:

* raw newbie
* start-up
* seasoned pro
* overworked pro
* growth business.

The aim is get to "seasoned pro" with minimum fuss, and avoid overshooting into "overworked pro." If you're ambitious, you can also investigate what it takes to become a growth business.

Raw newbie
No previous writing experience.
If you've never written before, you need to be realistic. Most of the professional copywriters I know have degrees in language, literature, sales or marketing, or are trained journalists, or subject specialists in a technical area. Others get into copywriting via professional blogging. So although it's possible to learn the art and craft of copywriting through hard work and commitment alone, be aware you'll be competing with writers who already have those kinds of skills and experience. Can you see yourself in that professional context, interviewing people, meeting clients, turning in great copy to tight deadlines? If so, it's time to progress to...

Start-up
Entry-level copywriter with professional writing experience in another medium.
You've never written any marketing copy before, but you've written plenty of other things – fiction, journalism, scripts, blogs, press releases, user manuals. Someone, somewhere, has paid you to write – whether in a previous job, or as a freelance.

This is important. Paid writers in other media have demonstrable and transferable writing skills. If you've been paid by someone to

17

write, you have some credibility and the beginnings of a platform, which will help you to be taken seriously. It also gives you a starting point for testimonials and word of mouth, to start the ball rolling.

Early pro

First jobs under your belt, one or two clients.
Early pro stage means you've done the most difficult thing of all: you've hung out your sign, won your first client, completed your first job, invoiced and received payment. You've made a sale. This is huge. To run a writing business, simply repeat this step many, many times, gaining increasing skills and experience as you go.

If you're completely new to copywriting, this can seem daunting. When I first started out, although I had journalism and other experience, offering writing skills to business felt like a big leap. The difficulty was getting comfortable with my writing skills having a market value. Confident asking for money for something that came naturally. This attitude can get you into trouble! The earlier you start earning what you deserve, the better. For more about this, see *Handling Money.*

Ideally, you'll want to get you through "early pro" stage as quickly as possible, and onto the next stage: building a work pipeline as a...

Seasoned pro

Regular clients, good word-of-mouth, steady work pipeline.
Seasoned pros come in all shapes and forms, from the part-time writer who freelances for local businesses, to the high-end full-timer with full books and a national reputation.

"Seasoned pro" is the sweet spot. Most freelances fall into this category, and never go beyond it. If you can maintain a manageable work pipeline, and earn plenty to live on, with extra put aside for rainy days, then there's no need to expand. In this stage, you can earn a good living, achieve a decent life-work balance, and enjoy freelance freedom. The nuts and bolts of getting here and staying here are covered in **Part II**.

In the next stage, you may start to feel the strain as an...

Overworked pro

Great word-of-mouth, too many clients, full-to-bursting work pipeline.
Few people survive being an overworked pro for very long. You really don't want to get to the stage where you crack up, and need five weeks off to recover.

It's common, though, for copywriters to experience a "feast or famine" cycle, with periods of full-on grind, interspersed with times when they suddenly find there's no work coming in. This is because when you're working full on to meet a tough deadline, it's hard to keep the other plates spinning.

When I'm *really* under the cosh, admin, general tidying, shopping and eating fall by the wayside. If you're not careful, this can be followed by a massive catch-up, when you discover you've missed an important email with a lovely offer of work. Or a sudden deathly silence, because you haven't done any marketing.

Another "overworked" scenario is for time to fill with small, poorly paid jobs, leaving you unable to take on a big, meaty one. Strategies for dealing with this are covered in *Day-to-Day Workflow.*

And finally, if you get a taste for greater success, or world domination, you're looking at a...

Growth business

Your business wants to grow beyond just you.
There are many reasons why you may want to grow beyond being a sole trader, including ambition, overwork, a desire for company, and retirement planning. Or you may simply want a villa in the Bahamas (in which case you're probably in the wrong line of work).

A growth business is a new phase of the business life span. Enterprise bodies and funders treat growth businesses differently from sole traders and small start-ups, thanks to the potential for job creation. Growing your business also entails greater risks, which is probably why most writers remain freelance sole traders.

While a growth business is beyond the scope of this book, some specific strategies and considerations are covered in *Grow Your Business.*

PART II

Kit & Caboodle

Copywriters are the luckiest workers in the world. You need very little equipment to start a business. Just a computer, and phone, and access to the internet.

No massive overhead costs. No stock. No need for an office, landline phone, fast broadband or fancy gadgets. It's the low overhead business *par excellence*. So don't let "kit purchase" or "a room of my own" become an excuse for procrastination.

My advice is to skim this book quickly, then go out and get your first job. If you wait until things are perfect, you'll never get started. Lose your copywriting virginity, see if you like it, get over any money hang-ups, then come back, learn and improve.

 To get started right away, head for **Starter Projects** and do **Assignment 1**.

Welcome back! This chapter is about kit and office equipment. You don't need 90% of it to get started, but it will give you an overview of technical options and considerations. Here's your basic set-up:

- computer
- mobile phone
- internet.

If you have the budget, consider adding the following:

- black-and-white laserjet printer
- second monitor (ideally touchscreen)
- Skype headset.

As your business grows, consider adding other items further down the line. But don't rush in and buy loads of shiny kit. Weigh up everything against the vital issue of getting good value.

Most equipment is a wild overspec when you're at this "bootstrap" stage. Be warned that electronic gizmos have a habit of whispering "tax deductible." Don't listen! When deciding whether to buy, develop your business muscles by considering "return on investment" (ROI). In purely financial terms, will it really help? Will it speed up your work, or improve your efficiency and productivity? Will it improve your writing health and well-being?

For my situation, a decent chair, good keyboard and standing desk all make sense, and the investment has paid for itself many times over. But there's no point in paying for – for example – new office furniture, when second-hand bargains are easy to find.

Your situation will be different. Exercise your financial judgement, and don't listen to talking gizmos.

The rest of this section is an overview of my own setup and discoveries over the years.

Hardware

Computer

For preference, I use a laptop. This allows me to be flexible, present to clients using my own kit, and work anywhere: cafés, libraries, on the train, in the office and at home. I started with a very basic laptop, thinking all I needed was word processing and email, and everything else would be a distraction. However, software and aspirations have a way of expanding at breakneck speed. I now use Adobe Creative

24

Cloud, and edit video and audio on my laptop – something I didn't imagine when starting out.

So if you can, buy a fast laptop with a powerful processor, and the biggest RAM you can afford, preferably with scope for a RAM upgrade, and several USB ports. Most laptops now have an inbuilt webcam.

Keyboard

If buying a laptop online, test the keyboard at a computer store first. Keyboard touch is crucial for a writer, especially if you're a touch typist. I like the HP Envy series for their large keys, combined with light but decisive touch. The keys also have backlights for using in low light. The Microsoft Surface is small and light, though expensive.

I use a lot of keyboard shortcuts, never the mouse, and rarely the touchpad. The position and action of the touchpad and mouse clicks may be a factor for you. This is a personal decision, so experiment.

Keyboards get a lot of pounding, and the keys can wear out, or get damaged. I've replaced laptop keyboards several times, inexpensively and with great success. However, it's a job best left to the manufacturer, and may mean sending the laptop away for a few days. Bear this potential downtime in mind when buying a laptop, especially online. Synch your documents remotely (eg on Dropbox or OneDrive), so that you don't lose access in the event of computer downtime.

Touchscreen

Many laptops now come with a touchscreen. These are fantastic. They give you different options for interacting with the software, so they're especially helpful for combating repetitive strain injury (RSI), one of the hazards of writing for a living.

USB, DVD, CD and SD

Most laptops no longer have CD or DVD drives. If you haven't bought one for a while, don't be caught unawares. Large file transfer is usually handled using USB, SD cards or cloud storage nowadays.

Spare power cable

A broken power cable can put your workflow at risk, so this is an extremely useful backup. If you work away from home, keep a spare cable at home. It'll save you carrying it around, and potentially damaging the connector.

PC or Mac?

If you already have a Mac, lucky you! The interfaces are beautiful and intuitive, and the keyboards have a nice feel to them. Despite secretly coveting a Mac, I use and recommend a PC for copywriting. Here's why:

The business world of PCs

Most businesses, schools, the public sector and charities use PCs, and the Windows platform. Microsoft Office is by far the dominant software. If you're a fluent Windows and Microsoft Office user, you'll automatically be compatible with most of your clients, and shouldn't have any problems. It makes business sense to accommodate your clients' workflow, rather than expecting them to adapt to yours.

Although not as glamorous as Macs, PCs are much cheaper and easier in terms of hardware, workflow and compatibility. Windows computers are everywhere, so if you're away from the office or your system breaks down, it's much easier to log on and use other people's computers. PCs are also cheaper and easier to upgrade with new components.

The creative world of Macs

Most graphic designers use Macs, which are perfect for visual work. Many other creative collaborators also use the Mac platform, including web designers, photographers and filmmakers.

In practice, designers who use Macs need to be "bilingual," as most of their clients typically have PCs. Mac-using web designers usually also have a PC for checking website performance across platforms.

In summary

While I'm not suggesting you throw out your lovely Mac, be aware that most clients will expect you to handle PC formats as a matter of course.

Occasionally, working between platforms can cause formating issues (such as extra spaces) in text documents. Check what platform your client is using – you'll occasionally encounter a client who tries to edit your drafts on an iPad. If you need to work with a different platform, stick to RTF document format.

Phone

It's best to have a separate phone for business, to keep a clear demarcation between your work and personal life. If you just do occasional freelancing and have tolerant clients who know you well, you can get away with only one phone line. But if you want to come across as a committed professional, you need two separate numbers. Clients are generally very nice people, but when it comes to spending their money on your services, they want your undivided attention. If they get the impression you're juggling domestic issues, a cat and an unruly child alongside their do-or-die marketing campaign, they may choose to go elsewhere.

Landline or mobile?

There are pros and cons to each. Location, signal, cost, image and your working habits all need to be weighed up. Convergence of technologies and increased use of Skype also mean the situation is evolving all the time. Here's where things stand for now:

Mobile

In the creative industries, many freelancers opt for mobile phones, and no longer have landlines at all. A mobile number will disguise the fact that you don't live in a city. It can also suggest that you're technically adept and switched on. With mobiles, you don't need to pay extra to see the caller number. Consider getting a dual SIM card with separate numbers for work and personal life.

Landline

A dedicated landline will reassure clients that you're a bona fide business. It suggests that you have an office, a degree of scale and solidity, and are going to stick around. If your clients are traditional or old-fashioned businesses, this may be an advantage.

If you use a landline, choose cordless, so that you can walk and talk, find files and access equipment without getting tangled. Make sure it has a hands-free speakerphone function, as you'll often need to type while speaking to a client. A Bluetooth headset is another option here.

Don't use your home landline. Family members can undo all your carefully built professionalism in an instant.

In summary

It depends on your situation. I have an office landline and broadband to keep business separate, but have considered switching to mobile dual SIM and VoIP (internet phone) to help cut costs. Search for "home business phone package" to check out the latest options.

Printer

Even if you aspire to a paperless office, you'll need a printer for documents. You may need printouts at short notice for clients. I also find proof-reading much more accurate when done on paper. Printers themselves aren't that expensive, but the cost of refills – especially colour – can be high.

Black-and-white printing

My biggest printing requirement by far is for superfast, cheap drafts for proofing, and occasional printouts for clients. Two-sided (duplex) printing is a time-saving and paper-saving must. I use a Brother black-and-white laserjet as my workhorse printer.

A printer with Wi-Fi capability is incredibly useful. Once set up, the printer can be plugged into any electrical socket within range. Wi-Fi is perfect if you need to work in a different office, or take the printer on holiday. Once it's set up to work with your laptop, you can simply unplug and replug the printer in the new location.

Second printer-scanner

If you can stretch to a second printer, consider one with a scanner-copier function. This can replace a photocopier for small numbers of copies. If it has Wi-Fi, you can set it up to email scanned documents directly from the printer. If you don't have a scanner, photograph documents on your mobile using a scanning app.

Colour printing

Colour laser refills are very expensive, and colour inkjet quality isn't that great. For colour print jobs where you need better quality, avoid the expense of buying a printer by going to your local college, library or print shop instead.

Other Equipment

These items aren't vital, especially when starting out, but can make a difference to your workflow. Before buying, ask whether they add real value to your business.

Second monitor

If funds are tight, invest in a second monitor, rather than a colour printer. You may already have a spare one belonging to an old PC.

When copywriting, you constantly need to switch between windows to compare copy versions, read source material, and research websites. It's so much easier with a second monitor hooked up to extend your main screen.

If you're buying a new monitor, go for a large touchscreen. You'll be able to use it for several programs at once. I use a second monitor to keep multiple windows open side-by-side. It saves switching, speeds up my process, and helps to protect against RSI.

Sit-stand desk

Depending on your space and budget, and any back problems, a sit-stand desk can be a worthwhile investment, especially as they've come down considerably in price.

The sit-stand mechanism lets you change positions during the day, relieve pressure on your back, be more active, and renew your energy and concentration when you get tired. I've found that this works brilliantly for admin tasks and phone calls, but not for writing itself. Once again, this is highly individual. If you can, try before you buy.

Fax

These are pretty well obsolete, except in law firms and government offices, and businesses needing signatures for legal or security reasons. Digital scans and signatures offer an alternative.

Photocopier

Domestic photocopiers have come down in price, but are still expensive. I still haven't seen the need to buy one, even though there's no copy shop nearby. A decent black-and-white laser printer can quickly run off 50 copies for a talk or workshop.

For bulk copying, it's cheaper to go to a photocopying or digital printing service, especially if your documents need to be collated or in better quality.

 Moneywise:

Libraries and colleges often offer photocopying services more cheaply than traditional copy shops.

Webcam

Most inbuilt laptop webcams are fine for Skype calls. However, the lens height of inbuilt webcams makes them less than flattering, and the inbuilt microphone is too far away to give you good quality sound. If you want better visual quality, eg for recording video interviews, you may want to invest in a separate USB webcam with a good quality lens.

I use a Logitech Pro wide-angle USB webcam, which gives good quality images and basic sound. For better sound, go for a microphone headset (eg Plantronics).

Microphone headset

A good quality one can be used for Skype calls, and also improves dictation accuracy if you're using DragonDictate. If you plan on walking around to retrieve files while on a Skype call, consider a Bluetooth microphone headset.

Hands-free phone or headset

When speaking to clients, you'll need to take notes and go online, so it's useful to be able to make hands-free phone calls. Most phones have a speakerphone or hands-free function.

If you often take notes on the phone, consider a separate phone headset – the kind used by switchboard operators. Or use Skype and a headset for client calls. It'll sound better than speaking down into a phone on your desk.

Software

Microsoft Office

Microsoft Office is a must. It's by far the most common software used by businesses. Microsoft Word is efficient for word processing, and has useful keyboard shortcuts that will speed up your work, and help prevent mouse-induced RSI. Clients often use Excel and Powerpoint, too, so you may as well get the whole Office suite. Rather than buying the software, sign up for Office 365 – it's cheaper, comes with access to new apps and Teams, and you get automatic updates.

Workwise:
Useful but lesser-known Word shortcuts
To highlight text, select then: CTRL+ALT+H
To insert a comment: CTRL+ALT+M
To toggle letter case: SHIFT + F3 (repeat)

DragonDictate

DragonDictate is a powerful dictation software program. It has improved a great deal in the last few years, to the point where it now copes well with my Scottish accent, and has become a useful copywriting tool.

It's brilliant at complex technical vocabulary, which it understands much more readily than everyday speech. It's also great if your topic is repetitive and calls for long word strings. DragonDictate works with Microsoft Word and Outlook, and can also be used with Scrivener.

DragonDictate is a huge help if you suffer from repetitive strain injury (RSI) or carpal tunnel syndrome. Even if you don't, your hands will soon complain if you start typing 1,000 words an hour, five days a week. RSI can be highly debilitating and recovery long, so don't ignore early warning signs, or you may find yourself unable to write at all.

Note that DragonDictate is expensive and memory-hungry. It's great for first drafts, but not so great for editing, which you'll still need to do by hand. The "dragon" needs to be trained to suit your voice and dictation style, which takes a little time. Before investing, check that:

- your computer is powerful enough to handle Dragon comfortably
- you have a decent microphone headset to give your Dragon quality audio.

32

Workwise:

You can use DragonDictate with mobile phone recordings made while out and about, as long as the recording conditions are reasonable. To do this, dictate into your mobile phone using any recording software. When you're back at the computer, hook up the phone and import the recorded audio file into your computer using the DragonDictate "Transcribe" mode. This will transcribe your audio automatically.

Scrivener

Scrivener is a word processing program loved by many writers – particularly novelists, academics, and anyone composing long, unwieldy documents. Its distinctive feature is the ability to chunk text into small sections ("scrivenings") and move them around easily.

Whereas with Word, you need to cut and paste *words*, with Scrivener, you drag around the *sections*. This makes it easy to organize a long text, capture stray thoughts, and generally write in a more intuitive, less linear way.

Scrivener truly comes into its own for long books, particularly if you need to gather research, references, and glossaries in one handy place. Some writers find it complicated to learn, and prefer a simpler visual interface. But it's so inexpensive that you may want to check it out anyway.

Adobe Creative Cloud

Adobe is the gold standard software for many creative businesses, whether in graphic design, layout, video or sound editing. Popular Adobe programs include Acrobat (for PDFs), InDesign (print layout), Premiere Pro (video editing), and Audition (sound editing).

Rather than buying these applications individually, creative agencies usually subscribe to Adobe Creative Cloud, an online subscription version of Adobe Creative Suite. Copywriters don't need this expensive software, but it's useful to be aware of the main Adobe applications you may come across:

Acrobat

If you've opened a PDF, you already have Acrobat Reader, which is a free program that can be downloaded from the Adobe site. PDF stands for "portable document format," and was designed as a cross-platform standard for documents. In other words, it can be used by both Windows and Mac.

Print proofs are usually supplied as PDFs. I always request a PDF copy of print jobs, to check for glitches.

InDesign

InDesign is a layout program used by graphic designers to create print documents such as marketing brochures, leaflets, and annual reports. It's also used for book and magazine layout.

InDesign is complex, and has many brilliant features you'll never need as a copywriter. However, if you do a lot of print work in collaboration with graphic designers, check out...

InCopy

InCopy was designed to enable remote collaboration between designers and copywriters. It allows writers and editors to work on the same document as the designer, at the same time, without messing up the InDesign layout.

This makes it particularly valuable for proofreading. It saves the laborious stage of PDF markup, or minutely listing the changes you want the designer to make. InCopy allows you to simply go into the document on the server, and make the text changes yourself, while protecting the design. If you don't have Adobe Creative Cloud, it's possible to subscribe just to InCopy, for a small monthly payment.

FreeAgent

FreeAgent is online accounting and invoicing software designed with freelancers in mind. Many people in the creative industries use FreeAgent, because it's highly visual and intuitive. It also provides great graphs and reports, so you can see your unpaid invoices and looming tax deadlines in glorious technicolour.

FreeAgent includes time tracking (for client hours), invoices, and a business dashboard with an overview of your financial picture. It even handles foreign currencies, VAT, employment and payroll, should you ever grow to that point. Tax returns can be submitted online through the program.

FreeAgent has simplified my financial management no end, and the customer service from professional accountants is excellent. There's a free trial, then an annual fee if you sign up. I swear by FreeAgent, and you can get a 10% discount by using my referrer code: 3y41i55a (**www.freeagent.com**)

Toggl

Toggl is an online time tracking programme which is simple and intuitive to use. The free version is enough for most users. Toggl helps you to understand how you spend your time. I use it to log client hours and my own work process. It has made me face up to procrastination and other freelance demons, and single-handedly improved my productivity by around 200%. It's also great if a client ever challenges you on time spent. You can produce a detailed time log in seconds. (**www.toggl.com**)

Microsoft OneNote

OneNote is a free program within Microsoft Office. It's essentially a virtual notebook where you can keep notes, images, tasks and recordings. You can also record audio and video within the program itself.

The real beauty of OneNote is that it lives online, and can be used by several people. It's a fantastic collaboration tool, intuitive to use, and ideal for gathering and planning. I use OneNote to manage tasks and projects, and share notes and to-do lists with clients.

Office Stationery

Office organization is highly personal, and what works for me may not work for you. As I'm not naturally organized, I've had to develop an effective workflow. Here's my system:

Diary

I use a day-to-page paper diary. It makes commitments seem more real, and doesn't have a layer of technology to get through before finding what you need. I also use Office Outlook as a digital backup which can be accessed from anywhere, and has links to information such as client phone numbers and maps. Belts and braces!

Wall planner

I use a whiteboard wall planner with a month's view. Calendars showing a whole year don't provide enough space for notes. A month also feels like a more graspable time unit for goal-setting.

Whiteboard paper

Whiteboard paper is a great alternative to solid whiteboards. It's a very thin plastic that clings to any wall, without pins or adhesive, and comes in a roll. I use this for brainstorming, and keeping deadlines in view. It's also useful for presentations, as you can prepare sheets in advance, and stick them up on the wall at the venue.

Labeler

Labeling folders, boxes and power cables keeps equipment and files in order, and makes it harder to lose things. If you'd find a labeler useful, get an inexpensive battery-powered one (eg Dymo). A couple of label refills should last for months.

Wallet folders

For each client, I have a labeled cardboard wallet folders that takes A4 paper. The client's business card is clipped to the front of the folder, along with any extra phone numbers, email and passwords needed (typically for development sites or social media). This makes key information easy to find, and means there's no need to open Outlook or Dropbox.

Workspace

You don't need an office to run a copywriting business. One of the great joys of writing for a living is that you can do it pretty well anywhere.

That said, I've found separate office space to be crucial. It keeps clear boundaries between work and personal life, and stops them from getting entangled. For me, it prevents chaos, stress, and distraction.

A separate office space also puts clearer boundaries on your time. Otherwise, you're a sitting target for any odd jobs that crop up, whether taking in parcels, or tidying the house. From there, it's a small step to a lack of recognition and respect for your work – by you or by others.

The other main reason to have a separate office is to get out of the house. Even if you're an irascible hermit, allergic to other people, and secretly happy to avoid them, social isolation is bad for you. It's bad for your soul, your mental health, and your ability to go out and connect with clients. So ultimately, it's bad for your business, too. If you can, find an office space to call your own.

Habits Audit

Before deciding on your own office, experiment and do a habits audit to understand your working preferences. If you haven't worked for yourself before, these will naturally evolve, but it's still worth thinking things through at the start. As before, what works for me won't necessarily work for you.

Do you prefer to work in silence?

As someone who's worked in a busy newsroom, with televisions and radios blaring round the clock, I know I do my most productive work in silence. Although I eventually got used to the noise, and it was sometimes exciting and stimulating, it was also distracting. These days, I work in glorious silence.

Do you enjoy chatting?

If you love a good chat, having people around can be problematic. You may also find visitors dropping in, seeing you as available for casual chitchat which can easily gobble up time. If you do work with others around, try industrial earmuffs. They're cheap, and last forever. In shared workspaces, they also give a clear signal that you don't want to be interrupted.

Do you have weird habits?

Let's face it, we all have weird habits. If they're likely to embarrass you, then working with others isn't a great idea. When I'm writing, I sometimes walk around and talk to myself. That's what I need to get into a flow state, but it'd be a bit awkward to have witnesses!

Do you work best under scrutiny?

Studies show that we work harder when someone's watching. It can make you feel more accountable, and boost your productivity. Test this out by working in a library. If you get loads done, it's likely you perform best with a degree of scrutiny. If you're on your own, pin a picture of a pair of eyes to the wall. Psychological studies show it helps.

Are you messy or controlling?

These opposite sides of the tidiness spectrum rarely get on well together in an office. Know thyself.

Office Options

One great aspect of the freelance copywriting life is that you have so many different workplace options. As well as working from home, you can also work in libraries, cafés, freelance hubs, house-sits – and mix it up if you get bored. Especially in cities, you can increasingly also find business hubs for creative and tech freelances.

So the situation is evolving. We no longer need to choose between a home office, and an expensive rented office. There are many shades in between. Here are the pros and cons of the main ones.

A corner of the kitchen table

Even if the Brontës got away with this arrangement, don't go there. You'll spend a lot of time in your chosen space, so it's best to have somewhere dedicated and business-like, both for your own organization, and for when clients come calling.

A dedicated workspace also expresses your degree of commitment to your work. A leisure or family space gives it marginal status in your life. At the very least, do yourself a favour and set aside...

A room in your house

Virginia Woolf famously suggested that writers need "a room of one's own." For a copywriting business, this is a must. Compartmentalising is crucial when working from home, otherwise you'll feel "always on," and never fully relaxed.

A dedicated room in your house, with its own desk, phone and bookcase, will also do wonders for your focus, and stake out your territory and intentions. If your territory needs defending, consider putting your business name on the door, and installing a lock. Use a separate phone line to keep clear water between family and business life. A dedicated home office also lets you write off a chunk of domestic heating and electricity, as well as some furniture and fittings.

People with large gardens sometimes opt for a separate home office. They're expensive but tax-deductible, and add value to your home. If your plans to sequester the spare room meet with opposition, mention the potential tax breaks.

Separate premises

A separate office outside your home is a big step. Many highly successful copywriters never go this route. That said, a separate address can provide a sense of scale and longevity, which may help to reassure clients. With so many high-street shops, offices and industrial estates lying empty, it's also increasingly possible to find low-cost office spaces. So the transition to dedicated premises may not be as costly as you think.

Here are some options for away-from-home offices, with pros and cons:

Creative sector hub

Creative freelance hubs are becoming increasingly popular, particularly in urban areas. They range from open-plan hot desks to individual small offices, and can be hired on a long-term basis, or for as little as a day. Large creative hubs typically have shared facilities, meeting rooms, and break-out spaces.

Some of these hubs are run by creative collectives, who can benefit from joint marketing and public tendering. Others are run by property developers, who are starting to value the sustainability of multi-occupancy over all-or-nothing bigger tenants.

If you can't find a creative or small business hub in your area, you may be able to find enough like-minded colleagues to start one. Let your local enterprise body know you're looking for shared office space. There are likely to be others in your position.

Business centre

Most towns and cities have business centres with offices to rent. These can be helpful for getting to know clients, and gaining a foothold in your local business community. If you share the building with other businesses, you'll be the natural first port of call for their copywriting needs.

Enterprise hubs sometimes offer incentives to start-up businesses, particularly if they're new to the area. This can include a first-year rent reduction. Some new businesses rent office space in a business centre for a year or so, to build their profile and win some clients, then move on to somewhere less expensive.

Business hubs often provide internet, utilities and receptionist services as part of your rent. If they're short of tenants, you may be able to negotiate a good deal. Before deciding, weigh up whether the other tenants and the location will bring work your way.

Solo office on the high street

With so many empty premises on the high street, it may seem obvious to look for an office there. However, most ground floor high-street premises are zoned for retail. Also, professional services (accountants, legal services, etc) typically prefer not to be *too* visible, as passers-by dropping in for a chat can stop them from getting any work done.

So a high-street presence would be an unusual choice for copywriters. But look out for this changing, as local authorities investigate new ways to fill empty commercial property.

Business incubator

Some enterprises bodies and banks run business incubators. The idea is to support ambitious start-ups by providing shared facilities, business and legal advice, and the opportunity to network. Other tenants will come from a wide range of business sectors, giving you a good chance of meeting new copywriting clients.

Often, these workspaces are offered free, or at reduced rates. The idea is that you stay for a limited period, benefiting from the bank's start-up advice, and move on to your own premises once established.

This is a formal business arrangement, so you'll need a business plan, and a clear commitment to developing your business. If they're going to invest in you, they want to be sure you're serious. If copywriting is just a sideline for you, or you don't have growth plans, a business incubator may be overkill.

Voluntary sector hub

The voluntary and community sectors often employ short-term project workers, and spaces can become available when projects end. My first solo office was in a voluntary sector hub. The building was home to projects including local transport initiatives, community support, and grant advice. Shared facilities included photocopier, internet and kitchen. Once again, assess whether the co-tenants are potential clients for your services.

Indie small business hub

This is simply an entrepreneurial version of a publicly subsidised business hub. My copywriting business, Texthouse, is based in an old textile mill bought by a local entrepreneur. After years of standing empty, waiting for a big business tenant, it's now home to over 50 small and micro-businesses. Joiners, car mechanics, textile artisans and designers work side by side with a gym, a dance studio, band practice rooms, and artists' studios.

This mix has been perfect for me. It doesn't have the swish facilities of a public sector enterprise hub, but doesn't have the high rents, either. It's also great to be part of a local regeneration project, with a community of supportive people and lively activity.

Roving Copywriter

One of the advantages of being a freelance copywriter is the freedom to work where you like. A setup designed with cloud-based file storage and email means you can work from anywhere that has Wi-Fi access. Try out different spaces for fun and variety. If roving works for you, you may not need an office.

Libraries

City libraries have a long tradition as a remote office for writers. The British Library gave birth to major works by George Orwell, Karl Marx, and Virginia Woolf, so why not you?!

University and college libraries can be inspiring and relatively quiet places to work. They also have desks at a good height for writing and typing. They usually offer internet access, and cheap photocopying and stationery. Cafés or canteens are close to hand. Private individuals can usually join as a reader, and access services for little cost.

Smaller town and community libraries can be noisy, with busy front desks, mothers reading aloud to children, and people watching videos. This makes them less useful as a regular workplace, but worth bearing in mind as a backup for internet and photocopying.

Cafés

Cafés can be fun places to work in, as they're full of life, and have great coffee on tap. There are even studies suggesting that a low level of café noise is productive for concentration. That said, cafés have disadvantages. Firstly, coffee is expensive. Secondly, cake and other temptations are easily available, and you'll probably over-order to assuage guilt about sitting there for hours.

But the main drawback of writing in cafés is ergonomic. The average table height in cafés is too high for writing, and can very quickly lead to RSI, or a painful back and shoulders. It's probably best not to use cafés as your regular office, unless you combine it with walks and stretching.

I write in cafés as a treat when I want to get out, meet other writers, and eat cake. For hard slog such as editing, I sometimes go to a nearby college library.

Remote working

With a work setup entirely online, you can turn nomad, and take your business on your travels. Copywriting combines well with self-catering, house sitting, Air BnB, and other good-value accommodation.

If you do this, make sure you'll have access to a decent internet service and phone, and have a backup plan, particularly if heading to a remote location. I once planned a remote house-sit, with acres of glorious time for solid research and editing, and the phone line broke just before I arrived. No comms for two weeks!

If you're planning to combine work and holiday with friends or family, be especially aware of the potential pitfalls. Don't take along a big or urgent job, in the mistaken belief you'll be able to fit it in. Even small jobs become hard to face in holiday surroundings. Traveling companions won't be thrilled to have their holiday mood disturbed by your work anxiety, and you'll resent them for going off on lovely trips. Or (more likely) you'll end up downing tools.

As with workspaces, it's probably best to compartmentalize work and play, and plan a proper holiday when you can truly relax.

Training & Learning

Workwise:

When starting out, you're in a chicken-and-egg situation. How do you get experience without being able to prove your abilities? Do an apprentice job for free. See **Starter Projects**.

The best way to learn copywriting is on the job. Get that first job out the door, learn from it, rinse and repeat. This means jumping in before you're completely ready.

As you'll find out, getting friendly with this kind of risk is central to business. The world is a shifting, ever-evolving beast. If you wait for the right time or try to perfect sure-fire strategies, you'll miss the boat. Everything will have moved on, and you'll be left behind.

If you're a perfectionist or risk-averse, you may want to follow a more systematic approach, do some training, and draw up a business plan. Just don't let this be an excuse to procrastinate on the real work of making a living. Set a time limit for your start-up. You can always do highly focused training later, when you know your exact needs.

Here's an overview of training and support options you may encounter, with pros and cons:

45

Training

Don't spend a fortune on training courses before you've done a few practice jobs, and worked out whether copywriting is for you. If you do invest, make sure you'll get enough value from the course to justify the time and expense.

Avoid training that doesn't fit your freelance situation. Courses designed for employees in the corporate world tend to be expensive, and usually aimed at marketers, rather than people with advanced writing skills. Make sure you're the right market for the course before signing up. There are some great books and online courses out there which are a better fit for creative writers and journalists. For useful links, see the **Resources** section.

Copywriting skills

Small budget/DIY
Read all you can by Andy Maslen and Steve Slaunwhite. See the recommended reading in **Resources**.

Online
For free basics focusing mainly on digital and SEO, see Copyblogger (www.copyblogger.com). For a general online copywriting course, see Andy Maslen's *Copywriting Academy* (www.copywritingacademy. co.uk). Read his books first!

Face-to-face
Face-to-face copywriting training providers include the UK's Chartered Institute of Marketing (CIM). I took their introductory course when starting out, after searching on the internet. However, it was aimed at junior marketers working for large companies and local authorities, and wasn't that useful. You'll pay a lot less for a well-targeted online course. The writers' organisation 26 sometimes runs courses for copywriters (www.26.org.uk).

Business and marketing skills

Small budget/DIY

Work through this book for a general introduction aimed at writers without a business background. Meanwhile, check out your local enterprise body for free introductory courses where you may also meet potential client businesses.

Read Peter Bowerman's *The Well-Fed Writer* or Steve Slaunwhite's *The Wealthy Freelancer* for an overview of financial management for freelances.

Face-to-face

Local enterprise bodies, such as Business Gateway in the UK, usually offer free basic business workshops. These typically cover topics such as marketing, business plans, and social media. For the equivalent enterprise body in your own country, search online for "business start-up" and "enterprise start-up" with your country name.

In my experience, enterprise workshops are usually geared to larger businesses, and aren't an ideal fit for consultants, freelancers and small creative businesses. But it's still worth attending these workshops, to familiarize yourself with enterprise concepts, terminology, and ways of thinking. It'll help you understand the client perspective better, and is also useful for networking, and raising your profile with the enterprise body, for potential referrals.

In Scotland, where I live, the Cultural Enterprise Office (CEO) offers basic courses in business skills for creative people. Their target audience is people in the creative arts and industries. They also offer 121s on the phone. The UK National Union of Journalists (NUJ) also offers professional development courses in topics such as PR, pitching and negotiating.

Online

If you're an NUJ or Writers' Guild member in the UK, the Federation of Entertainment Unions (FEU) offers business skills courses, face-to-face and online (www.nuj.org.uk, www.feutraining.org.uk).

Massive Online Open Courses (MOOCs) run by universities often include business topics such as digital marketing and bookkeeping (www.coursera.com, www.futurelearn.com, www.openlearn.com). MIT also offers short free entrepreneurship courses to participants all over the world at their online academy (www.edx.org).

If you're tech-minded, and want to go deep into SEO digital marketing, Google and Moz offer free analytics courses (www.moz.com).

Just be wary of disappearing down rabbit holes! For start-up, you can get by with what's in this book, and a couple of good copywriting books. Follow up on specific training once you need more depth.

Business planning

A business plan is scarier than it sounds. It's simply a map to keep you and your business on track. It's not essential, but helps to establish a benchmark, frame your goals, and set milestones to aim for. It's just a snapshot, and will evolve as you do.

If your business plan is just for you, then a back-of-the-envelope job is fine. If you want to apply for funding, you'll need to draw up something more formal, with financial forecasts, costs and goals.

Use a SWOT analysis to collect your thoughts, then fill in a business plan template. Search online for one, or try Microsoft Office, or your local enterprise body.

Business grants

When I started out, there were no grants for freelancer start-ups. However, the situation keeps changing. Try an online search for "business start-up grants." You may find some support for marketing initiatives or website development. If you do, weigh up the available amount against the time and effort needed to apply for it.

Business networking

If you're just starting out, you may be relieved to hear you don't need to go there – at least, not yet. For now, it's enough to print some cards and prepare an "elevator pitch" – a brief summary of what you do. If you venture forth into business situations, dress smartly and be friendly and human. For more tips, see *Business Networking.*

SWOT Analysis

A SWOT analysis (Strengths, Weaknesses, Opportunities, Threats) is a helpful decision-making tool. It lets you externalize your milling thoughts, to get a proper look at them. A SWOT analysis may seem like overkill when you're starting out, but as a freelance, you only have limited time. If you don't choose a path and follow it, you'll exhaust yourself following scattergun opportunities. So you need to be strategic.

A SWOT analysis can be adapted to different situations and stages. If you're a start-up, use it to gauge the best markets for your services. If you're more established, use it to understand where you are, and identify the best strategy for moving forward. The answers will be different for everyone. The point is simply to hold up a mirror, and analyse your situation more objectively.

Strengths
List your skills as a writer, and personal attributes. Work out what sets you apart from others, and might be a unique selling point (USP).

- What copywriting or journalism experience do you have?
- What portfolio evidence can you show?
- What markets and sectors do you already know well as a user?
- Any business or technical background?
- Any unusual experience in technology, IT, multimedia or engineering?
- Are you experienced at interviews, presenting, networking, training?

Weaknesses

Without beating yourself up, be honest about realities, and then brainstorm practical solutions.

- Do you need more confidence in writing for business?
- Do you struggle to explain what you do?
- Do you live in a remote area?
- Do you lack contacts?
- Do you handle your finances well?
- Do you struggle with technology?
- Do you need more understanding of marketing?

Now flip round your perceived weaknesses to identify any potential strengths. For example, if you live in a remote area with few potential business clients, maybe you can develop an international niche market, or digital marketing skills?

Opportunities

Brainstorm contacts and opportunities for finding work and building your network. Identify business developments and trends you've spotted, eg a new business park, a local video company.

- What makes you different to other copywriters around? What's your USP?
- What industries is your local area known for?
- Do your friends and family have potentially useful professional backgrounds?
- Might your previous employment provide some leads?
- What writing forms (eg scriptwriting, case studies) can you offer?

Threats

Consider obstacles to running your business: right now, short-term, and longer term. Again, exploring problems can help to highlight opportunities. Can you, for instance, compete with full-service marketing companies by teaming up with a graphic and web designer, and cutting out the middle man for print and web jobs? Threats may include:

- Companies cutting their marketing budgets
- Competition in your area
- Full-service marketing companies
- Online copywriting providers
- Lack of business experience.

Finally, highlight any findings that suggest themselves as a good way forward. Then, head to **Starter Projects,** and complete **Assignment 1.**

Launch

A posh champagne reception costs money, and your friends and family aren't your clients. What's more, it isn't real productive work, as it isn't billable. When starting out, you need to save your funds! These basic launch steps should cost very little, and take no longer than half a day.

Borrowing from the design concept of the "minimum viable product" (MVP), what's the minimum viable presence you need to get up and running?

- A name
- Business cards
- A one-page website.

Name
Business name or personal name?

Jules Horne, writer   This is clear and good to go.
Jules Horne, Texthouse   This is less clear, but I use it because it's:

- business-like
- confidence-building
- open enough to allow for other kinds of work (books, training...)

52

- larger-sounding than just you (useful, depending on your market)
- separate from your personal identity
- capable of growing beyond you.

If unsure, choose the first option. You can easily change it later.

Business name notes

Beware of terrible puns and words that will date or limit what you do (Carphone Warehouse, anyone?). If you're uninspired, search for "business name generator." It may be easier to start from what's available than spend days on creative agonising, and find everything's taken. Make sure your name also comes across clearly on the phone. Names with hyphens and oddities that need spelling out can become annoying.

If you can, choose a name that's available as a .com domain. These are much better for search than .net and .co.uk. Ideally, get .com and your national equivalent.

Business cards

Moo is simple, stylish, cheap, and allows short print runs. Use a clean design with no frills or clipart, and print the minimum number of cards (www.moo.com). A minimalist design leaves your appeal wide enough for clients in different sectors, as well as potential designer collaborators. Anything too fussy or quirky will limit your appeal.

One-page website

For getting started, WordPress (www.wordpress.com) and Wix (www.wix.com) are straightforward, good-looking and provide free hosting. Both can be migrated to your own domain name and hosting down the line.

For me, WordPress has the slight edge, as the platform is used by so many web developers. Familiarity with WordPress updating and its SEO requirements is also a useful skill for client work.

On your site, simply include your name, address and contact information, and what you're offering. Add a portfolio page if you already have something to put on it. Include your picture if you have a decent one, but don't let "no picture" stop you. Forge right ahead.

PART III

Build Your Business

With a few calling card jobs in your portfolio, you're now ready to go deeper into the operational side of writing for business. This section introduces some background context, as well as systems and kit to help you work more effectively. Even if you're already a seasoned pro, you should find plenty of ideas and productivity tips here.

What to Call Yourself

Earlier, I suggested that the word "copywriter" can sometimes cause confusion, and it may be clearer to say you're a "business writer," or that you "write for businesses." But job titles for writing services are changing fast. "Content writer" and "content editor" are now common in the digital world. So rather than confusing clients, first establish what line of business they're in, then adapt:

- IT and technical people are more likely to understand "content writer."
- CEOs and marketers: "copywriter. I write web content and marketing materials for businesses."
- B2B people: "writer for business. I specialise in (for example) web content and case studies."
- Creative sector people: "copywriter."

In the end, however, job titles aren't important. It's what you do for the client that counts.

Here are some strategies for finding collaborators and building your business.

Strategy 1: Creative Collaborators

When you start out as a writer for business, you quickly discover that certain key people are more helpful in fielding you work than others. These people are often your creative colleagues – professional web and graphic designers, and sometimes photographers. People who are creative, rewarding and fun to work with, and often have similar freelance issues to yours.

These colleagues are your new best friends (if they aren't already). In their own work, they regularly meet clients needing other creative services, including copywriting. At this point, word of mouth is everything. If you're on the radar as a reliable professional copywriter, and a good fit for the job, it's likely you'll hear about the work. And it goes without saying that this favour cuts both ways! See also **Complementary Businesses** and **Referrals**.

Here's an overview of your most likely creative collaborators:

Graphic designers

Relationships with graphic designers can be highly productive for finding work. Graphic designers typically work with a range of clients, at different scales and in different industries, and those clients often need copywriting services. Often, clients don't realize this, until the graphic designer tells them.

Graphic designers are also often the first port of call for clients who don't want the cost of a full-service marketing agency. Your services dovetail naturally. Just as copywriters love working with great designers who'll make their words look fantastic, designers love working with copywriters who bring the same care to their words.

58

Copywriter+designer is also a classic pairing in creative agencies. In the same way that musicians have favourite accompanists, designers and writers often pair up with others with a complementary work ethic, style or interests. A good working relationship between designer and copywriter leads to a better quality of work, and a more straightforward working process.

Web designers

Web designers often work with new clients who prioritize visuals, without giving proper thought to content. The clients may not have a plan for what to fill the site with once it has been built, or assume the old content can be migrated. This is an opportunity for you.

But before emailing all your local web designers, vet them properly. Not all web designers are created equal. As with all creative services, there are no barriers to entry in web design, and no quality control. Look for creative partners who match the quality of your copywriting work.

Small-scale

The sweet spot for you is small companies with a graphic designer, web developer, and possibly SEO or digital marking specialist. That way, clients get the best of both worlds, and your copywriting skills fit in beautifully. Companies at this scale are also more likely to attract bigger clients who see a greater need for marketing, and are more likely to have the budget for copywriting.

Web design companies which are sole traders tend to fall into two distinct categories: visual design-driven and technically driven.

Design-driven

Web designers from a graphic design background are more likely to build good-looking sites, with high-quality branding, graphics, styling and photography all helping to make the company's products and services look more valuable.

Sometimes, however, design-driven sites can fall down on the technical side – for example, with unwieldy graphics, or by

59

sacrificing sales impact and user experience to aesthetics. Under the bonnet, they may also be less attractive to search engines.

Technology-driven

Tech-based web designers are often excellent on the technical and data side of the website, including SEO, reliability and security. Their technical knowledge and lean, streamlined code may help a site to be found more easily on the web. However, tech-led sites can fall down on the design side, sometimes with clunky looks that make the company's products and services less attractive to customers.

Even among technology-led web designers, you'll encounter different approaches:

- those using commercial, ready-to-go templates
- those using established platforms such as WordPress or Joomla, with or without templates
- those coding sites from scratch, using html, php and Java.

Clients are often unaware of these differences, and sometimes pay a hefty rate for a cheap template site.

A vast portfolio of websites for small companies is usually a sign that a web developer is using templates. Typically, this kind of company attracts cost-conscious clients who may not have the budget for copywriting services.

SEO and database-driven

Big sites of high complexity are often database-driven, and SEO may be baked into their design from the start. Some SEO-driven websites put less premium on design and beautifully crafted copy. But you may be lucky, and find a highly skilled SEO team who combine high-level tech expertise with great visual design.

If you write for this kind of company, they'll probably provide you with an Excel spreadsheet of target keywords for each page. Your job is to write stylish content that connects with customers, and disguises its SEO provenance.

Finding creative collaborators

When looking for web design companies to approach:

- Check out the web designer's portfolio and clients.
- Look at the scale and type of business, and the design quality.
- Ask yourself whether your business will be boosted by association with their work.

Other considerations

Is the company using templates with poor design values? Chances are their clients have a small marketing budget, and aren't a good target for your copywriting services. Even if you can help to transform their clients' businesses, they may not want to pay what you're worth.

If the design is unattractive and out of date, but the company sizeable, they may be considering a new one, so now could be a good time to get in touch.

To grow your client list in a better-paid direction, focus on finding one or two high quality web designers for long-term collaboration.

Strategy 2: Marketing Agencies

For SME clients with reasonable budgets, the first port of call is often a marketing agency. However, small full-service marketers typically don't have the full spectrum of services in house. It's more usual for them to pull in contractors on a project basis, including web designers, graphic designers, photographers and branding specialists.

In my experience, small marketing companies rarely pull in copywriters or social media specialists, preferring to write clients' copy themselves. If approaching them, you may be perceived as direct competition. If making an approach, sound them out carefully and tactfully, rather than plunging straight in with an enthusiastic bid to take over their business.

Digital marketers

Digital marketers include traditional marketers gone digital, and digital natives with SEO and social media expertise. They are typically newer and younger than traditional marketing agencies.

If you're interested in SEO content writing, digital marketing agencies may be a good fit for your services. They're often run by people with tech skills and little writing experience. However, they may also view writing as a commodity, and their rates can be low. Digital agencies I've worked with have often fielded small jobs with tight parameters. Unless you're looking at high volume work, other areas may be better paid.

Strategy 3: Word of Mouth (WOM)

Word of mouth is the best kind of marketing. To be honest, it isn't really a strategy – it's a business basic. Develop a good reputation, and others will recommend you to their clients, giving you a steady work pipeline.

If this is already happening for you, great. If not, help things along by asking for referrals, testimonials and credits.

Referrals

In business, "referral" means a recommendation. As soon as you feel comfortable and have some jobs under your belt, start asking clients for referrals. This is common business practice, so rest assured that you're not doing anything unusual. If your clients have enjoyed working with you, and you've done a good job for them, they're usually happy to help. The world of business is surprisingly karmic. Helping each other out is one way for people to stay in contact.

Testimonials

Testimonials are essentially written reviews provided by your clients. Most clients are happy for their testimonials to be used on your website and print promotions, and may be willing to add a testimonial on the business social media site, LinkedIn.

A good time to ask for testimonials and referrals is when you've just signed off on the job, and have sent your invoice in. Hopefully, the client will be at a stage between delight at your work and guilt that you haven't been paid yet, and send you one by return. If not, follow up a couple of weeks later with a gentle reminder.

Make a habit of asking for a testimonial after each job completed. If your client is pushed for time, offer to draft it yourself, and email it for their approval.

Companies in sensitive sectors may be happy to provide an anonymized testimonial, eg showing their initials or job title, instead of a full name. In the interests of fair representation, if you need to shorten a testimonial, use ellipses, like this: [...]

Credits

Where possible, ask for print and web credits on client work. If they mention the designer, they should be happy to mention you, ideally with a link to your site. A site or brochure credit amounts to free advertising, and is well worth having, especially if it's a high profile, great-looking job you're proud of.

With websites, be aware that clients will change copy once it's up. If you're credited as copywriter, this can backfire if later writing isn't up to your standards. You have a choice here: either keep an eye on the website, and let the client know if anything needs to be tweaked (a good way to keep in touch). Or use a pristine screengrab on your own site, and don't link to the client site.

Strategy 4: Networking

For some people, "business networking" conjures up a nightmare: loads of suited men, juggling a plate of food/glass of wine, mumbling about exports, and avoiding spitting crumbs. This is only partly true!

If networking fills you with dread, don't despair. Many copywriters do just fine with clients coming to them. Once you get your first gig and good word-of-mouth, your work pipeline will start to build. Before you know it, you may have more than you can deal with.

So don't feel networking is something you have to do. Go with whatever you find comfortable. A decent website backed by LinkedIn and e-bulletins can go a long way.

If you do venture forth into business networking, don't be put off by the first event you go to. Look around. You may find a group that's a good fit, and enjoy yourself immensely.

As well as traditional business organizations such as chambers of commerce, increasingly you find niche networking groups for creatives, women and the self-employed. Some will suit you better than others.

But first, an explanation of networking, and why it's not what it seems.

The loneliness of the long-distance business owner

Running a small business owner can be isolating. You may have no one to talk to or discuss your problems with. The buck stops with you, which is a huge responsibility, especially if you employ staff. This is one of the key reasons why business people do networking. Not because they're "working the room," "rubbing shoulders," or doing any of the things writer-introverts recoil from. It's because they need to get out there, and see some supportive human faces on occasion.

So look on networking meetings as a water cooler for the self-employed. Or as a gathering of friends you may end up working with. Empathize with the problems and stresses small businesses face. This makes networking much easier.

Earn your chops

Just because you're a wonderful writer doesn't mean everyone will love you in this new environment. In any new endeavour, you have win your chops, by doing great work, and earning great word-of-mouth. Until you build a track record in copywriting, and can talk about businesses you've helped, you haven't got standing in that world.

Once you have a portfolio of clients, work will start to come to you. This takes time. So at your first few meetings, it's best to watch, listen, learn, and help where you can.

Sales culture

Many popular business books – the kind piled up at airports – have a sales orientation. They're often geared to the American market, and tend towards psychological techniques, sales tactics and a general air of can-do exuberance.

At a UK business networking event, this behaviour could get you arrested. If you treat people as "prospects," they'll run a mile, and your word-of mouth will be far from positive. So don't be misled. Many of these business books come from an increasingly outdated sales culture. Sales and marketing experts have realized that in-your-face selling is a turn-off. Consumers are increasingly immune, and even hostile, to these techniques.

Instead, challenge yourself to tune into the culture of each group you meet, and note its unique codes and language. This is good practice for the empathy needed to write for different sectors and audiences. And if you ever find yourself channelling Salesman Gil from *The Simpsons,* or anyone from David Mamet's *Glengarry Glen Ross,* give yourself a stern talking-to.

B2B beware

Business networking groups attract a lot of B2B suppliers – that is, people offering business-to-business services. That includes web designers, accountants, solicitors, marketers, PRs, and copywriters.

So you may find other businesses slightly suspicious. They can spot sales techniques a mile off. Come on too strong, and you'll put them off. To get round this, do a free talk for your local business group.

They'll get a sense of you and what you do, and may come up to talk to you at the end. If not, don't worry. You don't need to appeal to everyone. Just a few clients who are really in tune with what you do.

Is it worth it?

Business networking is a long-term game. You may be lucky and pick up work right away. It's more likely you'll find some contacts, get on someone's radar, and be remembered next time they need someone who can write.

Most business organizations and networking groups cost money to join, with extra for business dinners, breakfasts (yes!), and other events. Many groups let you go along a few times as a guest, to see whether it's for you. So there's no need to sign up right away. Look out for interesting speakers on their events programme, get in touch with the chair, and go along as a guest. Before joining as a member, put on your business hat, and weigh up whether it's worth your time and money:

- Are the members in your target market?
- Will having their logo on your site help you get more business?
- Does the group promote member businesses, eg links on their website? (good for site rankings)
- Are they friendly, welcoming, and helpful to you as a new business? (good for morale)
- Do they have a "buddying" system for new members (a good sign)
- Do you enjoy their company?

Membership benefits

Many businesses join a national membership organization solely for the insurance and legal benefits. You may not be interested in networking or advocacy, but you definitely need insurance coverage.

66

I'm a member of the Federation of Small Business in the UK, because they offer insurance coverage, as well as a free legal hotline. If you ever have an insurance or legal claim, your costs are covered, which is highly reassuring. See *Insurance* for more about this.

Sector trade groups

If you have a sector interest (eg tourism, food & drink, tech, textiles), look out for specialist trade groups. Some of these strategic groups are regionally based, with the aim of boosting that area of the local economy. Others are national or even international. Get on the group's mailing list for updates, and follow them on Twitter and LinkedIn to keep up to speed with sector news.

Trade shows

Trade shows are also a good port of call if you have a specialism, and some portfolio projects in that industry. It's a chance to do valuable research and trend-spotting, as well as networking.

Trade shows can be expensive, so go there with a business hat on, and clear strategies and targets for what you want to achieve. Take along sample materials, leaflets and cards. To gauge interest generated by the trade show, set up a landing page on your site, and give this out as your site address.

A sector specialism can be effective, as you won't need to research from scratch with each new client. But do avoid conflict of interest, and writing for companies that are in direct competition.

Niche groups

New kinds of business networking are springing up in the meantime.

Creative industries networking groups are a good bet for copywriters, as they attract graphic and web designers, photographers, and other creative specialists, who may want to link up for projects. You may find you're perceived as competition by other copywriters, but the more experienced ones will be happy to meet others with high standards, in case they need to pull in help.

Examples of UK creative industries networking groups include Creative Edinburgh, and the Creative Industries Networking Group (CING) in Manchester.

4Networking was designed as a refreshing antidote to traditional business networking, and prides itself on being unstuffy, fun and welcoming. It has a lively speed-dating model. It's expensive, though – go as a guest!

Women's business networking groups are usually friendly and inspiring, and may hold talks and presentations. Examples include the Women in Business Network (WIBN).

Export clubs are rarer, but worth investigating. Members usually have overseas backgrounds, and are open-minded and interesting. Examples include the East London Export Club and Scottish Borders Export Club.

Networking tactics

Don't talk about your business. Instead, ask others about theirs. Find out what they do, where they're based, how business is going, who their customers are. Don't "sell" yourself. You could come across as pushy, and possibly desperate.

Business networking is a long game, so establish yourself as friendly, helpful and knowledgeable. Always be prepared to give before you get something back. If you can give advice from your writing expertise, all the better.

And finally

Everyone you meet has friends, family, and colleagues who work in companies that may need your services. If they're not decision-makers themselves, they still influence what their bosses get to hear about.

So make sure they know what you do. Mention jobs you're working on. It's not blowing your own trumpet. It's just making sure you're on the radar when they need your services.

Strategy 5: Cold Calling

You'll be relieved to hear that you don't need to do any cold calling, ie unsolicited marketing calls. Cold calling has never been popular, whether you're a caller or a recipient. Unsurprisingly, it has the highest rejection rate and lowest sales return of all the marketing techniques. Cold calling is sometimes also used by scammers, and is governed by specific regulations in many countries. With the advent of the internet and digital marketing, it has plummeted further in popularity.

Just bear in mind that if you're tempted to drop by your local industrial estate for a friendly chat, brandishing leaflets, that's essentially a cold call. Busy businesses often don't want unexpected callers disrupting their day, and would prefer you to make an appointment.

Strategy 6: Digital Networking

Digital networking is a powerful alternative to word-of-mouth and face-to-face networking. If you're comfortable with social media, particularly LinkedIn, this may be a better use of your time.

At a minimum, have an up-to-date LinkedIn presence. This is where businesses of the scale you need hang out. A simple Google+ presence is also a good idea, as it can be powerful in search engine rankings.

Facebook, Twitter, and other personal social media are less relevant to business, though client businesses may be on here. I don't use these platforms for business, as they're a lot of work, and blur the distinction between business and personal life.

Email bulletins are a good way to help keep client contacts fresh, and drive traffic to new content on your website. You may want to set up a newsletter to grow your email list, and keep in touch with clients on a regular basis. Mailchimp is free to start with, and relatively straightforward to use.

With all these strategies, weigh up the return on your investment of money and time (ROI). Some ways of promoting business are more effective than others. Only use social media and digital marketing if you enjoy it, and can do it quickly and efficiently. Otherwise, it can quickly overwhelm you, at the expense of productive work.

Strategy 7: Complementary Businesses

Look out for "cascader" or "influencer" businesses that complement yours. As well as other creative businesses, consider working with other businesses and organizations with good client contacts, often providing business-to-business (B2B) services. The key factor is that your services don't overlap, and you're not in competition.

Complementary businesses may be happy to provide informal leads or referrals, sometimes in exchange for a referral fee. They may also be open to cross-promotion of each others' services, whether through word of mouth, or reciprocal website or social media links. Potential cascaders include:

Accountants
Accountants have a wide range of business clients who may need your services. Your best bets are likely to be locally based. Like web design companies, accountants operate at different scales, and with different kinds of clients. Get a sense of whether their clients are a good fit for the kind of work you want to do.

Enterprise bodies
Local enterprise organizations often work with start-ups who need copywriting services. Publicly funded bodies aren't allowed to recommend preferred suppliers, but they can get around this by suggesting a shortlist of providers. Make sure they're aware of your services, and your target market.

Other B2B services

Many B2B services are in niches where their clients may need copywriting services:

- Wedding planners work with hotels, caterers, florists, photographers, and many other suppliers.
- Catering equipment companies work with restaurants, bars, care homes and works canteens.
- Dental kit and software manufacturers work with dental practices.

With these potential partners, be clear about the market, scale and kind of client you typically work with. Develop a few good B2B contacts, and you'll never be short of work.

Business Concepts & Culture

If you're a newbie copywriter without a business or marketing background, you'll encounter lots of unfamiliar concepts and terminology when starting out.

This section is an unapologetically eclectic gathering of the concepts I've found useful. Some are about business basics, other about culture or preconceptions. Many business terms are now in widespread use as general metaphors, but have a specific meaning in their original context. A question like "who's your market?" sounds simple. In practice, it means understanding concepts such as demographics, geography, distribution, scale, and value. If you're coming at copywriting from a creative writing or arts angle, as I did, this is where you need to put some work in.

Who's Your Market?

When I first launched my business, my market was "anyone in my area needing copywriting services." Obvious, right? Wrong! A "market" needs to be closely defined, or you'll have a scattergun business that lacks focus, and attracts unfocused clients.

As it turned out, the area I live in wasn't a big enough market to sustain my business. There weren't enough potential clients willing to pay a good rate for my services. I *could* spend time trying to "educate" clients about the benefits of copywriting. But it would very labour-intensive, and they still might not value my efforts. My early scattergun approach put me on the radar of lots of clients with tiny jobs (editing leaflets, press releases), which ultimately wasn't productive. You may (like me) be happy to do this kind of job to support local companies, but it will never earn you a living.

What's a Market?

"Market" is one of those words that's so widespread in general use that it has almost lost its meaning. However, understanding markets and market segments is the key to making a living from your writing.

Markets are places where buyers and sellers meet. Where like-minded tribes gather to exchange goods and services. But when you imagine a marketplace, what comes to mind?

- A rough-and-ready bunch of Saturday stalls in a car park?
- A farmers' market with a tiny range of artisan products?
- A shiny city mall full of chic boutiques?
- A school tuck shop where kids can sell their home-made cookies?

These are all markets. They vary hugely in scale, demographic, complexity, and competition. Similar products are sold very differently in different markets. You can buy pretty much the same jeans from a market stall, a shop, or a bijou boutique, at wildly diverging prices.

Different kinds of buyers and sellers frequent these niches or "market segments." This is vital to an understanding of who might pay for your copywriting services.

Market segments

Markets can be segmented in different ways: by scale, sector, specialism, distribution channels, and other differentiators. The crucial point is that you can't be all things to all people. If you want to write for the public or third sector, these are different markets to SMEs or craft artisans.

This is extremely helpful when it comes to your own marketing, and decisions about how to project yourself as a business. A quirky, creative website may be perfect for attracting other small creative businesses. But to someone in the public sector, it says that your market is "creative businesses." Conversely, if you want to work for creative artisan friends or for the creative sector, a corporate-style site will put them off, and may suggest you're too expensive for them.

It's crucial to recognize that there are no rights or wrongs here – just a recognition that you need to find the right market and tribe for the services you provide.

Target markets

When deciding on your target market for copywriting, potential differentiators include:

- scale of business
- B2B or B2C
- sector (finance, hospitality, etc)
- geography (local, national, international)
- demographics (young, old, male, female, etc)
- type of work (advertising, case studies, blogging, etc)
- marketing and distribution channels (online, office-based)
- type of marketing (digital, traditional, SEO)
- existing in-house copywriting capacity
- familiarity with copywriting as a service.

These categories intersect and overlap. You need to carve a space within this complexity, in order to structure and focus your efforts.

One strategy is to focus on a specific market segment, and exclude the others. Assess whether companies in that segment are likely to have the budget and motivation to pay for your copywriting services. Some small businesses may not even be aware of copywriting as a service. They just want to get their website up. In that case, it's fine to spend time explaining what you do. But if they need to be persuaded of your value, or prefer DIY copywriting, move swiftly on.

Words & Commodities

"Commodities" are reasonably interchangeable types of item which are relatively consistent in quality, such as coffee, sugar, petrol, and milk. Commodities are different from manufactured products, in that customers aren't typically concerned where they get them from, as long as the quality is reasonable. With commodities, people aren't brand loyal. They shop around. As long as they can find petrol, they're not usually too bothered about who's selling it.

So what's not a commodity? Everything that's not a staple item. Everything where the company and quality matters. Clothes, quality foods, toiletries, entertainment aren't commodities. Nor are words and creative services. Quality matters.

This may seem obvious, but it isn't always obvious to clients. Client businesses who haven't worked with copywriters before may be tempted to choose a provider based on price. They can't necessarily tell whether it's great quality.

You're a high-quality supplier. You need to find clients who appreciate the difference. Be wary of clients with a "commodity" or price-led view of copywriting services. If this is the case, they may not appreciate the quality of your work, and your value to them. Consider carefully before taking on this kind of client.

Customer Avatars

In marketing, "avatar" has a specific meaning. An avatar is a customer profile. Companies sometimes use customer avatars to get a better understanding of their target customers.

Ideally, a customer avatar is a specific real person who can be consulted, not a "type." The perfect avatar will be in the right target demographic, love the product, and be likely to buy it. Sometimes, that's the copywriter! In other cases, a customer avatar is a fictional character, with a name and detailed background. They're used to help marketing teams to focus their efforts, clarify their market and tone of voice, and make sure everyone is on the same track.

If you're a creative writer, you're used to creating and empathising with characters, and so this is familiar territory. Customer avatars might be way to reframe your creative skills for a business context.

Elevator Pitch

An elevator pitch is a brief summary of your business – one that ideally takes no longer than the 60 seconds it takes to go up in a lift with someone. That someone may be a potential client, or just a stranger who asks what you do.

"What do you do?" is a surprisingly common question, and can catch you unawares. If, like me, you're not very coherent in lifts, write out your elevator pitch and practise it till it's perfect. This will hone your business vision at the same time. Be prepared to evolve your elevator pitch along with your business, and adapt it to different situations.

One Way to Formulate an Elevator Pitch

Identify the customer and their pain point. ("You know when businesses commission a new website and struggle with what to put in it?")

Explain what you do. ("I take their raw information and write stylish SEO web content...")

Explain the value of what you do. ("...so that they get found easily on the web, and customers find information that helps them decide whether to buy.")

This is an SEO example. Depending on your copywriting niche and skills, you'll come up with something different.

Risk & Reward

We all prefer to work with people who are straightforward and 100% reliable. However, business is a fast-moving, chaotic environment. Risk goes with the territory. If you aren't happy with a certain degree of risk, then maybe it's best to consider whether business is really for you.

If you do corporate work, you'll encounter swish offices, boardrooms, suits, espresso machines, purchase orders, billing cycles, reception staff, and a job brief, which can be reassuring. But if you offer copywriting services at the pointy end of SMEs, you'll often encounter delightfully chaotic, disorganized individuals. You may visit messy offices, untidy shop floors and dusty backrooms, with the boss busy unpacking boxes, and mucking in with everyone else.

The backstage reality of small businesses, and especially start-ups, is eye-opening and fascinating. If you expect everything to be cut and dried, you're in the wrong line of work. If you're open-minded, inquisitive and interested in the Wild West of SMEs and their varied owners and workforces, then you might just love it.

So be prepared. If you aren't given a brief, get ready to step in, take charge, and negotiate one.

Mindset

It can take a little while for someone immersed in the arts or humanities to learn the business mindset. For me, a particular challenge was learning to be assertive about the financial value of my time. Another lesson learned was establishing clear boundaries between informal advice, and unpaid consultancy.

This can be a problem even for experienced consultants. Having clear policies and taking the lead will clarify things for both sides. You may not want to seem off-puttingly bureaucratic, but seasoned business people appreciate someone who respects their time. They will also spot a softy a mile off, and are unlikely to tell you if you're charging too little, if it means they're getting a bargain. If you have rhino skin, laser focus and don't take shit from anyone, you'll be fine. Just don't overshoot and become scary!

Collaboration

Creative writers, especially of poetry and fiction, are used to being in complete control of their work. They're answerable to no one, and that's how they like it. Copywriting, however, is a collaborative process, more like scriptwriting or editorial work. You need to be creative and flexible, solve problems, and not feel defensive when people prefer other solutions, or want to tweak your work. Any ego or preciousness needs to be left at the door.

With small businesses, your collaborators may extend beyond the immediate client to their team, board, or even spouse. Clients have even been known to sign off copy, show it to their mates, and come back with changes.

Set boundaries from the start of your client relationship by agreeing a process, including how many editing rounds are included in your service.

Iteration

"Iteration" is a concept often used in software development. It's included here because it's an excellent way to explain the creative process to technical people. The word comes from the Latin for "repeat," and refers to a cyclical development process of small actions, followed by adjustments. It's a way of making fast, concrete progress that adapts to changing knowledge and understanding.

Iteration is useful concept for business in general, and also for the writing and editing process. Some business owners don't get how the creative industries work, and don't understand that they can't just put in an order, and get a copywriting "product" by return. Inexperienced businesses may even wonder about your competence if you don't immediately produce a perfect first draft. They don't realize that it's a usually a two-way process of discussion, drafting, feedback, and editing, arriving at the final version in stages.

I use the term "iterative" to describe the creative process to technical people, reinforcing the point that it's non-linear. Engineers and software developers are familiar with this word, and it helps to manage expectations.

Hype & Spin

Writing for business isn't about hype or spin, hyperbole, or bigging something up to the point where it's unrecognisable. If a client ever asks you to be economical with the truth about their product or service, walk away. It isn't just unethical – it's also very hard to write positively and authentically about something you don't like. It'll quickly turn you cynical about the job of copywriting, and that's not a good way to spend your life.

By the way, this has never once happened to me. The reality is that most successful small businesses are based on a good idea, a good product, and good marketing, crucially backed up by good word-of-mouth. Particularly in this internet age, customer service and products have to be better than ever before. Poor word-of-mouth ensures that businesses are quickly found out.

So forget dated notions of "hard sell." Your role is to communicate authentically what the product can do for the person interested in buying it, and connect the potential buyer with the seller.

Tone of Voice

"Tone of voice" is a company's written personality. This is part of a company's brand, and is a strategic choice that needs to fit well with a company's visuals, story, strapline, and other brand and marketing parameters.

Ideally, tone of voice should be agreed at the start, as part of a company's brand strategy. With websites, however, copy is often considered late on in the process, and you may have to discuss tone of voice once company branding, photography, and even the development website are already in place.

In general, companies want to sound friendly and engaging, rather than aggressive or snobbish. But even within that framework, there can be tremendous variation, depending on the company's target market. Even a simple decision about whether to use direct address "you" has a substantial impact on how the company connects with customers.

Register is another important consideration. Vocabulary choice and energy also vary wildly. Think of the range of voices in TV chefs, from bubbly-zany to reassuring-homely to casual-laddish, and everything in between. And then there's the issue of the target customer's own culture, terminology, and any usage that can distinguish insiders from outsiders. Finding the right tone of voice needs careful discussion and research.

To do this, first establish the client's target market, customer, and typical user. Are their customers teenagers? Wealthy pensioners? Wind surfers? Dog owners? Think about age, sex, demographic, geography, social status and interests. Browse forums and websites to get a flavour of the vocabulary, register and energy they use.

Consider positioning. Is the client aiming for high end or mass market users? Is the product low cost, or expensive? All these factors have a bearing on tone of voice.

Before embarking on a whole website project, write a few samples in different tones of voice to illustrate the possibilities. Check out what the company's competition are doing. Ask the client for their views on use of direct address "you," and how they describe their customers (service users, clients, subscribers).

Run these options past the client and reach a consensus before starting to write. Nailing the tone of voice from the start will save a lot of editing later on.

Branding

Branding is a specialist area of marketing. It calls for higher-order conceptual thinking, and covers overall vision, tone of voice, metaphors, and intangibles such as look and feel, as well as visual design work. Bigger companies can spend a lot of money on branding in this wider sense, and this work is typically done by a creative agency, in partnership with the in-house marketing team.

However, small companies often misunderstand branding, and designers often get asked for "new branding," meaning simply a new company logo and colours. Copywriters can then be asked to "come up with a strapline" to go with the new logo. This shortcuts a vital thought process, and misunderstands the true power of a brand. You're being asked to express a vision, values and voice which the company hasn't yet properly articulated. Clearly, this is the wrong way round.

If this happens, ask whether the company has been through a branding process, and remind the client that your strapline will be visible on company banners, vans and stationery for years to come. At the very least, consult with the designer, provide several alternatives, and get a good hourly rate for this service.

Immersiveness

Creative writers are familiar with the distinction between "immersive" writing where the words disappear, drawing readers completely into the "fictive dream," and writing that draws attention to itself and the author's voice. So where does copywriting stand on this continuum?

How we engage with writing is of course very personal. The top creative agencies often win awards for clever copywriting that shouts "look at me." However, copywriting isn't about the copywriter. Its aim is to sell a product or service. If people are detached enough to notice how clever the copy or ad campaign is, they may not notice, remember or be emotionally engaged with the product itself.

Creative writers are ideally skilled to appreciate that difference, and write copy that engages customers and invites them into a world, rather than showing off with verbal pyrotechnics. The *Innocent* fruit drink campaign is a good example of a "look at me" writing style that won awards and inspired a host of imitators. In its day, it was exceptional, but customers quickly adapt to the new, and the exceptional can eventually become commonplace and even clichéd.

These different approaches aren't bad or good. Like "showing" and "telling," they're simply different techniques that have different effects on readers in different situations. Which brings us to...

Show & Tell

Creative writers are familiar with the difference between "show" (illustration) and "tell" (straight facts). In fiction, "telling" is sometimes portrayed as the bad guy, but this is misleading. Sometimes readers are impatient and just want the facts. Other times, they want description or dramatization, for a sense of immersion, atmosphere or tension. "Showing" and "telling" have different uses and effects. It's the same in copywriting.

By and large, "telling" comes first. Especially on the internet, people are usually scanning for information, and want it fast. A list of product features and benefits is a quick, straightforward way to get a message across. Describe what a product is, what it does for you, and why people buy it, and you won't go far wrong. The downside of telling is that it can sound too "salesy," and potentially off-putting. Customers may also be sceptical of claims without back-up.

"Showing" is a more sophisticated, less direct way of getting a message across. Showing a product or service being used is a powerful strategy that's often played out in product photography – especially lifestyle images. It provides evidence that the product is valued by others, and allows customers to identify with the user. It gives them a point of connection with the product and its world, and a space to imagine. In a way, this is the copywriting correlate of the "imaginative gap" familiar from creative writing.

Creative writers are intuitively familiar with showing, telling, and the psychology of engagement. An understanding of how this translates to the marketing context is extremely useful for copywriting.

Storytelling

A few years ago, not many businesses had heard of "storytelling" as a marketing strategy. Now, the "story" metaphor is ubiquitous, and "narrative" is a buzzword. People are more aware of how narrative can be used to powerfully shape perceptions, whether in films, politics or marketing. So, businesses understand the need to "tell a stronger story," which is great news for writers!

Why is storytelling particularly engaging in business? Because good stories are relatable, and involve transformation and evolution, so they harness our senses of empathy, curiosity and possibility. At some level, we transport ourselves into the story, and feel its transformational journey.

Skilled storytellers have an advantage over copywriters from a marketing or technical background, as they're familiar with the tools and techniques of storytelling. Characters, tension, secrets, metaphors, reversals... they can all be harnessed to use in your copywriting.

Case studies, for example, can be framed as stories with central characters. Brands can be built on a strong central metaphor or image, which can be followed through in copywriting. Look out for storytelling techniques used in marketing, and opportunities to adapt your existing skills.

Jargon

People often mock jargon. But every sector has its special ways of talking – even writers. One person's jargon is simply another's handy conceptual shortcut. In business, specialist terminology is simply how an industry talks to its itself and its market.

Once we understand that jargon is a badge of shared values and interests (in linguistics, a "discourse community"), it stands to reason that it isn't innately bad or wrong. So it's best not to judge it, as this can come across as ignorant or arrogant.

But clients sometimes don't appreciate how deeply they're steeped in their sector terminology. They may be too close to their work, and take it for granted that their language is widely understood. As a copywriter, you're in the ideal position to step back, identify with the customer, and question anything that seems obscure. This can be an eye-opening experience for companies.

Getting the language right for a specific niche is delicate work, and if you get it wrong, it'll stand out a mile. Step into the customer's shoes, and work from there. Try using verbatim techniques to "harvest" a customer group's vocabulary and style. It's a great way to hone an authentic voice and character, and useful for expanding your voice range in creative writing, too. Ask your client – or one of their customers – to check your copy for inconsistencies.

84

Women in Business

Successful women in business are now highly visible in the media and everyday life. Women's instinctive strengths of team work, collaboration and communication are increasingly recognized and appreciated. Women's entrepreneurship is growing in the UK, and research shows female-run businesses have better survival rates during recession than those run by men.

That said, some business sectors are more conservative than others, and may have few female role models. You may even encounter sexism from unenlightened individuals. Don't sweat it, and don't get upset. It's not worth your time or energy to battle years of ingrained views. You won't succeed, and will only deflect time that should be put into productive business. It's best instead to concentrate on people you instinctively gel with, and who get what you do. If you can't find them, you're looking in the wrong place. Cast your net wider. Look out in particular for creative sector hubs, and women's business networking, which are usually welcoming and supportive.

Dress Code

In theory, there isn't a dress code for copywriting. The freedom to wear what you like is one of the great joys of the trade. But when it comes to meeting clients, it's time for a rethink.

Dressing smartly is simply a way to show respect to others. You value their time, and the opportunity to meet, and demonstrate this by making an effort. However, creative businesses do enjoy some leeway, and people don't expect pin-stripes and ties. Smart casual will see you through most situations.

If you're attending a formal business meeting, think "teaching job interview." Wear something that gives you a sense of authority, and wouldn't distract or diminish your respect in front of 15-year-olds. If in doubt, ask a teacher.

Day-to-Day Workflow

Once you've done some calling card or apprentice jobs, and have a basic understanding of the territory, it's worth spending time putting an efficient workflow in place.

Work can quickly build, and once your job pipeline is in full flow, it's hard to step back and adjust. What's more, if you're a freelance, personal and work life can get very entangled. Clear systems will keep things separate, and help to prevent future headaches.

Over the years, I've tried various approaches. I've made loads of mistakes, and wasted a lot of time and money through inefficiency. Now I have good systems in place, my work life runs far more smoothly and productively, both creatively and in terms of income. So here are some thoughts. They're not the only way to do things, but they work for me.

Technical

This section covers the operational side of writing, including workflow. The "flow" metaphor (pipelines, blockages) is helpful not just for your writing, but also for working with clients. Sort out blockages, and work and earnings will flow more smoothly.

Systems thinking

Systems and routines can help you work more effectively. Creative people typically aren't systems thinkers, so you may find the idea unappealing. Maybe freedom from routine is the very reason you've embraced the freelance creative life! But after many experiments, I've realized that systems are essential.

When you freelance, work has a way of expanding to fit the available time. Deadlines seem somehow more negotiable, and if you fail to meet one, you're only answerable to yourself and the client, not your terrifying boss.

Creative people are also notoriously easily distracted into doing things that are more fun in the moment. Divergent thinking is, after all, is the very essence of creativity. So don't be surprised if you find the freelance life tougher than you thought.

Systems and routines can save a lot of time, by freeing up brain space to allow you to focus on the important and productive work, rather than the bittiness of everyday life. After all, brain work is hard. Even if you're sitting at a desk all day, thinking uses up a surprising amount of energy. If something can be streamlined and made simpler, it reduces friction in your mind – something known as "cognitive load." This is one reason why Steve Jobs always wore the same clothes, saving brainpower for his work. The phenomenally creative choreographer Twyla Tharp also talks about the importance of daily routines in achieving the right mindset for her dance practice.

So while you'll want to avoid being enslaved by systems, there are good reasons to corral unimportant jobs, to make room for what counts in any business: productive work that earns you a living. You probably have routines that work for you, and new ideas and technology are emerging all the time. If not, try some of mine as a starting point, and then experiment, observe, and perfect your own process.

Operations manual

An ops manual is simply a gathering of systems and routines you use repeatedly. I use a Word document for this, and add to it regularly. An ops manual can really help speed up your work turnaround. It helps prevent faffing, overwhelm, and energy wasted on unimportant things.

I use mine for processes, and add to it each time I do something new. That way, the process steps are captured, and I can forget about it until next time. This is amazingly helpful for technical info you don't need very often (eg image sizes for your website), and also for regular routines. Captured processes can include things like:

- ❀ new client onboarding
- ❀ settings for recording a podcast
- ❀ end-of-month bank statement reconciliation.

You can also include macros, keyboard shortcuts, useful checklists, and frequent travel information.

The beauty of capturing workflow is that you end up with a training manual to pass on to anyone helping you with your business. I've found this helps me to do repetitive jobs when I'm tired or under par, as I can simply follow the steps, without needing a huge amount of concentration.

 Workwise:

Try gamification. If the name *Operations Manual* is off-putting, call it *Secret Dossier* or *Magic Almanac* – whatever works for you!

Computer wrangling

 NB Computer hardware and software are covered in *Kit & Caboodle*.

This section is about computer routines to help your workflow.

Email

Don't use your personal email. Set up a separate one for work. As a freelance, there's enough blurring between your professional and personal life. It's best to minimize this where possible.

Ideally, use an email account you can access anywhere. This can be a life-saver if you're on the road, your phone runs out of juice, or your laptop is in for repair. I use Outlook 365, but there are many other options, including Gmail.

Browser setup

Save time by setting up browser tabs for pages you use all the time. Where possible, set them up to log you on automatically. My basic browser setup includes Toggl, Google, and website admin.

Use browser bookmarks and folders to organize frequently used sites. Mine include folders for my own sites, client sites and development sites, research and admin. When working on a website project, I also add clients' competitor sites and trade organizations for reference.

Passwords

Passwords can quickly get overwhelming. As well as your own passwords, you may have to manage client passwords, and access their development sites, e-bulletins and social media.

I use the password management software 1Password to keep everything together. It saves so much time, and also improves logon security, by allow you to generate and manage complex passwords. Once you've installed 1Password on your browser, simply enter a master password for access to all your logons.

Minimize distractions

If you're easily distracted, consider creating two different logon identities for work and personal use. Empty your desktop as far as possible, particularly if you use it to store memory-hogging videos and images. Everything on the desktop slows down the logging-on process.

Delete games. If you use Windows 10, remove all tiles that aren't relevant to work. Switch off tile animations and photograph streams. Switch off automatic always-on email. Instead, log on deliberately, a few times a day, to corral the time you spend answering emails.

Online storage

I keep all work documents online on Microsoft OneDrive (similar to Dropbox), synched with my local hard drive. This means everything can be accessed remotely or by a remote team, and files can be shared with clients. More importantly, if my computer breaks, I can migrate to another straightaway, without losing work, files and time.

It goes without saying that security is paramount for online storage. Don't compromise it by using a simple, everyday password. Back up mission-critical documents on an external hard drive.

Filing system

This is highly personal, and what works for me may not work for you. But you do need a process, or work will quickly get out of hand. Here's mine, to save you time.

In my online storage, I have a JOBS folder, and named sub-folders for each client. Each new client job or inquiry progresses through these sub-folders:

- ❖ INQUIRIES for inquiries, and quotes awaiting acceptance
- ❖ LIVE for client work in progress
- ❖ BILLING for completed, but not yet paid
- ❖ DONE for complete client projects.

This is backed by a parallel setup for physical folders:

- ❖ live projects go in cardboard wallet folders labelled with the client's name
- ❖ completed project folders are stored in box files.

Each new client gets a dedicated:

- online storage folder
- Outlook email folder
- cardboard wallet folder.

The wallet folder is used for papers, and for grabbing quickly to take to meetings. On the front, clip the client's business card, and on the inside, any URLs, logos and passwords you may need.

Other equipment

Printers, phones and other technical equipment can be complicated. If you're on the phone to a client, you may need to wrangle technology, find papers, take notes and speak coherently, all at the same time. It's amazing how stress makes mission-critical numbers – even your own phone number – vanish from your memory at a crucial moment.

To help with this, I put visible labels and lists where they're needed. Each time I find myself searching for something, this is captured, and a reminder put in the obvious place.

Workwise:

Post your phone number and postcode on the wall.

Post your Wi-Fi password on the wall, in case needed by visitors.

Stick instructions for printing envelopes and headed paper onto your printer.

Mark the "handsfree" button on your phone.

Emergency backup

Laptops have a habit of breaking down at the worst possible time. Have an emergency system in place, so that you can transfer to another computer quickly, and complete the job.

A second computer doesn't have to be a fabulous machine. A low-spec laptop is fine, as long as it has your main word processing and emailing software set up, and access to your passwords and online storage.

Other useful emergency items include a second power cable, in case the first breaks. It's also a good idea to carry around a high-capacity SD card or USB drive for transferring files onto another computer – particularly valuable for situations where a projector doesn't speak to your laptop.

Finally

Any time you notice yourself stalled, or unable to find or operate a piece of equipment, note the sticking point. Take a tip from the Japanese art of *kaizen*, and find a practical way to smooth the process, and cut down friction next time. Over time, these small steps will make your workflow more efficient, and save time and energy for the real work.

Writing

This section is a look at the writing process, with a view to understanding and streamlining your workflow where possible. Breaking down the different stages of writing and editing can help you identify bottlenecks, prevent overwhelm, and improve productivity.

Clearly, we all write in different ways. For many people, the writing process is organic, holistic and somewhat mysterious. If you have a process that works for you, and prefer not to analyse it, that's fine. Look away now!

I've found it helpful to use process analysis to understand the distinct stages, and how they relate to each other. They typically include:

* gather information
* organize
* formulate mentally
* formulate in writing
* line edit
* proof.

I discovered I spent a lot of time on research, which I enjoy and find interesting. However, many website copywriting jobs don't call for detailed research. You can waste a lot of time chasing down details, facts, examples and colour which the client already has on tap. So instead of sending the client a perfect first draft, I now send an imperfect draft, marked with gaps for them to fill.

Analysing my process also showed that even though I type fast, my typing speed was a bottleneck. I was also getting RSI from too much time at the keyboard. Investing in DragonDictate software has made a difference to both.

Whatever your process, see if it can be improved. New tools to make writing faster and more efficient are emerging all the time. Here's a breakdown of the stages in my process, to help with developing yours.

Gathering

In copywriting, certain documents and materials are useful as a research starting-point. Before a client meeting, ask them to provide:

- company vision statement (typically included in funding applications)
- current marketing materials
- links to a couple of competitor websites
- some examples of copywriting they like.

This helps to kickstart discussion around content, target market, and tone of voice.

Drafting

Websites have infinite capacity to absorb content, so it may be tempting to just start writing, and keep going. But in business terms, jobs without boundaries are a bad idea.

Think like a journalist, and consider the space and format you're writing for. Agree a specific job scope and wordage with the client. Do they need a 400-word blog article? A two-page case study? A

3,000-word report? A 30-second radio commercial? Deciding this at the start will help to focus your efforts, and manage expectations on both sides.

Some long-form writing such as blog posts and landing pages are typically broken down further with sub-heads [h2s]. These help with SEO, and with structuring your thoughts. User these headers where possible, to give extra clarity and structure to your writing.

If you're handling a long job with lots of elements, such as a website, write a couple of pages, and ask the client to check the tone of voice. Get this signed off before continuing.

Client reviews

Microsoft Word has a "Track Changes" function. Ask clients to click this and send back their annotated version. The number of review rounds should be set out in your terms and conditions, and agreed at the start. This will help to protect you from indecisive clients, moving goalposts, and scope creep. Client thinking and circumstances will inevitably evolve as a job progresses, but make sure there are clear limits, and that the client understands that you'll start charging extra if the job goes beyond what you've agreed.

Editing

For me, editing is the fun part of writing – it's where the magic happens. But it's easy to waste time by getting the different editing stages tangled up.

Big-scale structural editing is very different from close-up line editing and close proofing. Publishers deal with these different scales by dividing editing into different stages, with different editors responsible for each one.

This is a useful distinction in copywriting, too. Each editing stage calls for a different mindset. Structural editing calls for boldness and compartmentalising, while line edits call for a sense of logical and melodic flow. Proofing is all about tiny nuances and detail. Being clear about which stage you're on makes it easier to edit confidently and quickly.

Especially when starting out, it's good to remember that there are infinite successful ways to do every job. Don't get hung up on finding the perfect way in. Practise turning drafts around quickly and efficiently, and sending them out.

Proof-reading

Proof-reading calls for excellent eyesight and a degree of perfectionism. This is particularly crucial for print materials, which can stay around for decades. Clients often overlook tiny slips and typos, but customers may notice and pick up subliminal signals about lack of care, which undermine the overall quality message. It goes without saying that accurate, confident proof-reading is non-negotiable for a copywriter.

Other Skills

Other time-saving skills well worth acquiring include:

Touch typing

It's surprising how many people who write for a living can't touch type. It speeds your process up enormously. To me, it makes typing feel like playing an instrument, with intuitive flow between thoughts and the keyboard. Being able to type blind also liberates you from the strain of staring at a screen.

If you can't yet touch type, spend a week following an online training programme such as Mavis Beacon, which is fun as well as fast. It'll transform your turnaround speed.

Website updating

If you've ever blogged, you'll be familiar with the basics of website updating: creating hyperlinks, inserting and sizing images, adding pages. Website updating and other technical skills let you manage your own site, and save money. These skills can also give you an edge over traditional copywriters, who may be used to supplying just words.

If you can, learn your way around WordPress. It's the world's most popular content management system (CMS), and many web developers use it. Being comfortable with basic WordPress updating allows you to offer extra services, including blog updates and meta descriptions for SEO. Some clients may let you update their sites directly, to save them time (as long as you don't crash the site. See **Disclaimers!**). If you do offer extra technical services, reflect this in your rate.

Handling Money

Confident money wrangling is vital for business. Poor money skills can really come back to bite you as a freelance, especially if you get ill and can't work. A spend-as-you-earn habit can also get you in trouble when tax bills come in. Spare a thought, too, for later life, when you'll need savings.

Financial management for freelances is beyond the scope of this book. But do at least sort out the basics, and make sure you earn what you're worth. If this feels crashingly elementary, jump to the next chapter. This section is for people like me, who visibly quake at all things numerical.

Money & Creatives

Money can be something of a taboo topic among creative people. After all, we're artists. We pour our creative souls into every word we write. Money is the last thing on our minds, right?

Now that's out of the way, let's talk common sense. If you're not making decent money from your copywriting business, you're doing it wrong. It's a business, not a voluntary organization. This may sound obvious, but I'm constantly meeting creative businesses and freelancers who bust a gut for their clients. Meanwhile, those clients are zooming around in expensive sports cars, having glorious foreign holidays, blingy watches, and other trappings of success we can only dream of. And while we may not want those precise things, we do at least want the basics, including a roof over our heads, and food on the table.

Since money is an unsavoury topic, let's roll up our sleeves, and examine it closely. A healthy relationship with money, and sense of your own worth, will make your business life much easier. Confidence in handling money will also transmit to your clients in terms of professionalism. So it's important to get it right.

Systems

Systems thinking is hugely helpful for business finances. To keep everything clear, think of your freelance business as its own self-contained microsystem, entirely separate from your personal finances. Then you'll be able to keep track of how it's working for you.

To start out with, all you really need is a Excel spreadsheet that shows income and expenses. Send this and your receipts to your accountant at the end of the financial year.

Business bank account

If you're running a business, you need a separate bank account. Sometimes freelances, especially when starting out, think this isn't necessary. After all, as a sole trader, you and your business are the same legal entity, and your work and personal finances are closely entwined. But in practice, it's much clearer and less confusing to keep them separate. Starting your business finances off with a clean slate will also quickly reveal whether you're running things effectively.

Most banks are keen to attract new businesses, and offer information packs and business advice to start-ups. They usually offer fee-free services for the first year or so. Alternatively, some freelances use a separate personal bank account for work finances. Ask around, and find out what other freelances in your area do.

Book-keeping

Basic financial record-keeping is a must. Luckily, freelance copywriting is very low maintenance. The secret to book-keeping sanity is "little and often." Often, it's simply a case of inserting a few expenses and sending out a couple of invoices once a week.

To keep record-keeping under control, either update transactions right away, or book a dedicated hour in your diary each week. Stick to your commitment, and stay up to date. That way, the backlog won't build up, and turn into a monster that haunts your dreams. Most enterprise bodies offer basic book-keeping training to start-ups.

Most commercial accounting systems are wildly overspecced for freelance copywriters, who have few expenses and overheads. But many creative freelances swear by online accounting software specially designed for freelancers. I use FreeAgent, as it's intuitive and visually oriented.

Expenses

Expenses are stationery, premises, mileage, and anything else you need to carry out your business.

In freelance life, the territory between business and personal expenses sometimes gets blurred. For example, is that café meeting with your writing friend a business expense? The basic rule is: is the purchase necessary to carry out your business? If in doubt, it's personal.

With this in mind, it's easier to decide a clear demarcation in your head before a meeting, rather than afterwards. That way, you always know whether you're doing business. This also helps to focus the meeting, and encourages you and others to appreciate the value of your time.

Quotes, estimates, ballparks

Get into the habit of providing quotes and estimates quickly and systematically. It's a good idea not to waste too much time on them, as you won't get every job you quote for. Clients often pull in two or three quotes, especially if they're applying for grant funding.

Whether you're asked for a quote or estimate, scope out the work realistically, itemising where possible. This helps clients to see exactly what they're getting for their spend.

A quote is binding. If you supply a quote, you need to supply the services for the stated amount.

An estimate is informed guesswork. If the scope of work starts to expand, let the client know where you stand with hours, and clarify expectations on both sides. That way, if there's a limited budget, you can both agree to focus your efforts where they're most needed.

Quotes and estimates are usually valid for a limited period of time, such as six months.

A ballpark figure is more informal. Ballparks are used to scope out the rough territory, and check there are no unrealistic expectations on either side. A ballpark figure can help to establish that both parties are in the same market, with similar values. This early discussion saves everyone time and annoyance. Anyone put off by your ballpark figure is no loss. They're simply not in your target market.

Different industry sectors and scales have different payment terms – anything from "by return" to up to two months. My payment terms are two weeks, which is standard for small companies.

Project rate

Project or fixed rates give clarity to both sides, and are usually preferred by clients, especially for big jobs such as websites. One advantage of this is that as you gain experience, you'll get faster at the same work, giving you a bigger profit margin.

But there are also pitfalls. Client disorganization and unrealistic time estimates can lead to "project creep," where the work scope expands enormously. This is common with websites, which can absorb infinite amounts of content. In this situation, what seemed like a reasonable hourly rate can quickly shrink. You can end up shouldering the burden, and getting seriously underpaid.

To accommodate project creep on large projects, add a 10% contingency payment to your quote. Itemize the elements of the job (6 web pages, 3 blogs, 300 words), to clarify expectations on both sides. If you're asked for substantially more input, point out there are "cost implications," and charge accordingly.

Costings and estimates get easier with practice. While you're learning to judge this, log your time, and compare estimated with actual time for different types of job.

Aim to establish a "job" rate for different types of project – a 300-word blog, a four-page leaflet, and so on. Clients will appreciate the clarity. An upfront approach to rates also wards off anyone wanting to hire you too cheaply.

If the job is sizeable, ask for a 30% downpayment before you start, and send the client a letter of engagement to sign. Although this may seem formal, it's accepted practice, and secures commitment on both sides. It also means that if something goes wrong on the client side, at least you've been paid something.

Day or hourly rate

Time-based payment at a sensible rate ensures you'll be properly paid, and gets round the problem of project creep. If you go this route, clarify client expectations by giving a rough estimate and updates as you reach that amount. Keep a record of the work done, to show where your time has been spent. Make sure your hours are good value, and that your client isn't paying for you to learn on the job. If you're slow because you're new to the process or the industry, that's part of your development, and shouldn't be at the client's expense.

Whether to charge an hourly or day rate depends on the size of the job and, to an extent, the culture of the sectors you work with. Consultants tend to charge day rates, whereas trades tend towards hourly rates. Day rates can sound expensive, and put off clients with small jobs. Regular small jobs are good for cash flow. So a mix is good.

Big company, slow payer

Big companies and organizations are often slower at paying than small ones, usually because they have more bureaucratic procedures.

Payments are often dealt with in a big sweep at the end of the month. If you're unlucky, your invoice may narrowly miss a payment run deadline, adding on another six weeks before you get paid.

So if you're dealing with a large company or organization, be aware that payment can be slow. If this is an issue for you, ask about their payment terms, and if necessary agree an upfront payment.

Value added tax (VAT)

When starting out as a copywriter, you don't need to be registered for VAT (also known as "goods and services tax") in the UK. Unless you're earning more than the £83k VAT threshold, registration isn't necessary.

It's still possible to register voluntarily for VAT while under this threshold. Some businesses do this, so that they can claim back VAT on business purchases. However, the paperwork is onerous, and it's rarely worth it. Copywriters don't have a lot of expensive purchases, and anything that increases bureaucracy is a waste of time.

The time to look at VAT registration is when you cross the VAT threshold (or whatever applies in your country). Note that the United States and some other territories don't use the VAT system.

Retainer

Some copywriters are in the fortunate position of being "on retainer" with a client. This means you get a regular payment, in return for your commitment to providing regular services. This may arise with a regular client who wants your commitment on a project, but can't justify part-time employment or bringing you in-house. I've never worked on retainer, and suspect it's uncommon for copywriters working for SMEs. But it's worth being aware of, in case you're ever asked.

If you do a large amount of regular work for a client, the boundaries between contracting and part-time employment can become blurred. These roles come with very different tax statuses and employer obligations, so if in doubt, check with your accountant.

Letter of engagement

Get into the habit of asking clients to sign a letter of engagement. This may seem unnecessary, particularly if it's someone you know, where you have a degree of mutual trust. However, it's surprisingly easy to fall into doing free work. A chance meeting can turn into an offer to help, which turns into hours spent, and before you know it, you've done a chunk of work without being paid.

A letter of engagement is a good way to formalize the relationship, manage expectations, and establish that you're a serious business. It's an accepted part of business practice, and a company that refuses to sign one may be best avoided. This doesn't need to be overly formal. A simple email outlining your basic undertaking and terms is fine. If you deal with corporate clients, you may want to get legal advice and set up a template letter.

Accountants

Even as a micro-business, it's best to have an accountant. Although copywriting accounts aren't usually complex, working with a good accountant from the start means you always have a clear overview of what's going on in your business. It also gives you confidence that you're recording everything correctly, and not lining up any unpleasant surprises for future.

Although there are costs in hiring an accountant, in practice, their services work out as cost-neutral. You'll spend hours tearing your hair out, groaning and getting things wrong, whereas your accountant will turn the job round fast and accurately. It's also worth knowing that accountants feel as frustrated by amateur accounting as you do by amateur copywriting. Unless you're numerically gifted and motivated, hire an expert.

Accountants and accountancy rates vary hugely. Some aren't looking for business from small sole traders, and want bigger fish. If you choose the first accountant you come across, you may end up paying far more than you need to. So ask around for recommendations from other creative sole traders. Ideally, you want someone local you can trust

103

and get to know. Your relationship with your accountant can also bear fruit in other ways, including referrals.

Your local business support service may suggest a few names, though they usually can't give specific recommendations. Make clear that you're a sole trader with simple accounts, and don't need a big accountancy firm with swish offices.

Barter

Bartering is a great way to get started and build a portfolio. To "barter" is simply to exchange your goods and services for someone else's. Typical bartering scenarios might be:

- Write a graphic designer's website, in exchange for some great leaflet design.
- Write some marketing copy for a hair stylist's newspaper ad, in exchange for a fabulous haircut.

When to stop bartering? Almost immediately. Firstly, copywriters can't live by design, photos and great hair alone. You also need food, shelter, clothes and a bit more besides. And barter needs to work for *you*. The exchange needs to be something you really want.

The difficulty is that other businesses often underestimate the value of copywriting, and how long a good job takes. They may think that giving you a lovely hand-crafted necklace is ample reward for your 1.5 days of slog, when actually, five hand-crafted necklaces is nearer the mark.

They may also misunderstand the relationship as a friendly exchange, rather than business. So don't barter at all, if the transaction is in danger of being misunderstood. You may not get a choice in what you're offered, and haggling quickly gets awkward.

Also, be aware that the barterer may be a seasoned bad-ass pro, fully aware that they're getting a bargain. And if you're soft-hearted or apologetic in your financial dealings, they'll run rings round you.

It's far better to be upfront. Discuss your rates and quote a price at the start. Insist on a fair exchange, and don't feel morally pressured, just because you're selling time, and they're selling products.

Mates' rates

Mates' rates are useful when starting out, especially if you're working with a graphic designer or web designer colleague. Make it clear, however, that you're offering mate's rates, and aren't simply a pushover.

Business and friends don't easily mix. Difficulties can arise when you're asked to "cast an eye" over something, "pep it up" or (worse) "cobble something together." You see the draft. It's awful. You have to rewrite it, to save their business. But it takes hours. You expect at least a token payment. But somehow the question never arises.

Stay alert. The nicest people will try it on. *Really* nice people understand your time is valuable. Toughen yourself up by seeing your time in terms of its value in things or experiences. An hour's work may be the equivalent of a train ticket. A couple of days' work might amount to your rent.

Late payment

One downside of fixed rates for bigger jobs is that getting paid can take a long time. Once the work is underway, you may find yourself working long hours, and completion dates getting pushed back, still without payment. It's up to you to take the lead on this. If it's a big job, agree a 30% upfront payment. This establishes your business relationship on a clear footing, and signals commitment on both sides.

Occasionally, you may struggle to get paid. This can be for all sorts of reasons: because the client has a long payment cycle, because they have cash flow problems, or because they're on the point of meltdown. In this situation, you need to be quietly persistent, and make sure they know you won't back off.

Keep tabs on all your outstanding invoices, and follow up right away if you haven't heard from someone by the due date. If there's no action after your first gentle reminder, swiftly follow up with a stern one. If you don't get a reply, follow up on the phone. It may simply be that something has gone astray. At this stage, give the client the benefit of the doubt, and ask when you can expect payment. Confirm their undertaking by email.

In bigger companies, the person in charge may be on holiday, or the accounts department answerable to someone higher up in the chain. Showing respect and understanding to your contact in this situation can go a long way.

If you've tried these tactics in quick succession and still haven't been paid, it's possible you're being given the run-around. It may be that the company is juggling cash flow, or may be in trouble. At this stage, you need to decide whether to escalate. If you suspect the company is going out of business, it's important to take action quickly, or you'll be last in line, and may never get paid.

Membership of business organizations such as the Federation of Small Business (UK) often includes access to a free legal hotline and template legal letters. As a UK sole trader, you can also pursue debtors via the Small Claims Court, which has simplified procedures for small debts.

The alternative is to instruct a debt collection agency, who will send these letters and pursue the court claim on your behalf. This is relatively inexpensive, and will save you time and grief. It's also more likely to wake the client into action than a letter from you. Ask your local enterprise hub for a recommendation.

Of course, it's far better to pre-empt this kind of situation with a letter of agreement, and swift invoice follow-up. This won't protect you against client meltdown, but it will put you ahead of other creditors who are less organized.

In the end, though, these situations are uncommon. Mostly, business people are honest and pay their bills. With watertight systems in place and professionalism from the start, you'll usually head off such problems.

 Disclaimer:

This book doesn't cover legal processes. If you want legal protection, look into membership of your national small business organization, which may include a legal hotline.

Legal Nuts & Bolts

Here's a round-up of some basics points it's useful to know when starting out. Bear in mind, however, that I'm not a legal expert, and your situation will be different. When in doubt, seek independent legal advice.

Legal status

As a new freelance copywriter, you're most likely to start out as a sole trader. This means you're trading as a self-employed individual. You and your business are the same legal entity.

As a sole trader in the UK, you can still operate under a business name, or trading name. This gives you the simplicity of being a sole trader, with the extra impact of a business identity. In practical terms, simply clarify this in your self-employment tax return, eg "Jules Horne t/a (trading as) Texthouse."

If you grow bigger, or want extra legal protection, you may want to consider becoming a limited company, separating you and your business into distinct legal entities. "Limited" refers to limited personal liability in the event of something going wrong for your business. It means, for example, that personal assets such as your home are protected if your business gets into trouble. Limited status involves a much higher degree of bureaucracy and accountability to others. In the UK, private limited companies are registered with Companies House, which is a government agency.

Self-employment and employment

Most copywriters are self-employed. However, if you start doing very regular work for a client, you may unwittingly cross a line. If you're hired as a contractor, rather than an employee, the client can avoid statutory insurance and pension obligations. This may attract the attention of the tax office.

If you do occasional bursts of freelancing on and off for a client, that's fine. If the boundaries are blurred and you aren't sure that your self-employment status is correct, get legal advice.

Insurance

Copywriters need professional indemnity insurance to cover potential risks arising from carrying out their professional work. This includes situations such as a legal or compensation claim against you, based on the service you provided.

You may also need public liability insurance. to cover any accidents or damage caused in the course of your business activities. You'll want to consider contents insurance, to cover loss of equipment. If you employ people, you'll also need employers' liability insurance.

The good news is you don't need to set up each policy individually. Just search for a "professional insurance package" aimed at professionals and consultants. Your national business organization may also offer good rates for professional indemnity insurance, including a free legal advice hotline. The cost of membership is usually worth it for this service alone.

Take care that the insurance company doesn't categorize you under "journalism," as journalists sometimes attract higher insurance premiums. Insurance companies who are unaware of copywriting may try to put you under "secretarial." Suggest "marketing consultant" as a better fit.

Copyright

People can get very hung up about copyright and intellectual property (IP), but it's actually really simple:

- Don't steal anyone else's work.
- They mustn't steal yours.

That said, the freedom of the internet means the theft of your words may be a concern. Here are some practical tips:

Don't sweat it
The chances of someone stealing your copy are vanishingly small. Don't turn it into an obsession. Life is too short and court action too expensive to bother chasing. Send a polite email, ask them to stop, and forget about it. Unless they're actually selling tea towels with your work on it and making a fortune, it's probably not worth the bother.

How to handle copyright
My approach is simple: as soon as clients have paid my invoice, copyright transfers to them. That's world copyright, in perpetuity, across all existing platforms and those still to be invented. This serves three purposes:

- It encourages them to pay the invoice quickly.
- It makes them feel they're getting good value, as they can reuse the work on different platforms (print, web, advertising).
- It's legally clear.

Clients change your website copy
Clients will frequently change your website copy once it's up. Unless they make a mess of it and you use their site as a calling card, don't get upset. You're not being paid for the time it takes to monitor or correct their copy. If it's really bad, suggest it needs editing and offer a price.

Workwise:

Think of your copywriting as a beautiful jacket. As a couture jacket designer, you have no control over how customers will wear your creation. They may tweak it, stick pins in it, and take scissors to the hem. They expect to be able to wear it where, when and how they like. Let it go!

Promotional use of creative work

It's accepted practice for creatives to use client work to promote their services, eg in a web portfolio. It's good form to let your client know, and also any photographers and graphic designers involved, in case of objection. Usually, people are happy to benefit from the extra cross-promotion.

Clients lifting others' copy

It goes without saying that *you* would never steal anyone else's copy. After all:

- You're a better writer.
- Your clients are paying for fresh, original copy.
- Recycled copy will be noticed and penalized by search engines.

However, your clients may not be so straightforward. Take great care when asked to "give a onceover" to copy provided by clients. They may have patched it together from competitor websites. In this age of sharing, they may not even realize this is illegal. If the copy sounds suspiciously good or you spot different styles, ask the client where they got it.

Terms & Conditions (T&Cs)

Terms and conditions should be included on your website and letter of agreement for basic legal protection. They don't need to be complicated – just an outline of your payment, service and copyright terms.

On your invoices, refer clients to your website T&Cs. That way, you have some clarity if there's any dispute in future. There are plenty of example T&Cs on the web, but don't copy them – they're copyright! Draw up your own, and get them checked by a legal adviser.

Data protection

If you're in the UK or EU and hold data about your clients and suppliers, you need to comply with the General Data Protection Regulation (GDPR), and probably register as a data holder with the UK Information Commissioner's Office (ICO), for a small annual fee. To find out more, go to www.ico.org.uk.

Disclaimers

In your T&Cs, include a disclaimer stating that responsibility for the final copy rests with the client. This will provide some protection, in the event a zero has been missed from your client's annual report and causes a stock market crash. When a job or draft is complete, ask clients to confirm "sign-off" in an email, and send your invoice. This will force them to be decisive about completion.

To be clear, I'm not a legal adviser and have no legal training. So do your own research, and take legal advice on any T&Cs and disclaimer clauses you draw up. Neither I nor my heirs and estate are responsible for anything that happens to you as a result of following the advice in this book.

Working for Yourself

If you've never worked for yourself before, you're in for some big changes. But with self-employment on the rise, and more and more people taking the plunge into freelance life, it's no longer quite as tough as it was. There's more support around, and more understanding. There are even workplaces specially geared to this kind of working life.

There are many advantages to working for yourself. You're your own boss, and can choose your jobs, where you work, and who with. But this freedom also comes at a price. There's less job security, and it can be tricky if you get ill. Self-employment can sometimes be lonely, especially after the first couple of years, when the novelty has worn off. At least with a low-overhead business such as copywriting, you can try it out for a while, and see how you get on.

In some ways, freelancing is a throwback to ancient times, when our working and personal lives were very much interconnected. The village baker, for example, lived in the bakery, and didn't shut the door on neighbours who happened to want a loaf in the evening. This more holistic, less compartmentalized way of seeing the world suits many creatives. But combined with the creative strengths of curiosity, and divergent and imaginative thinking, it can cause problems, particularly when it comes to focus. Creative people can also be resistant to the idea of being corralled by work. These factors can make it harder for creative people to earn a good living as a freelance.

So, you do have to be tough about earning a living, and putting money away for rainy days and your future. Most of us also have to learn how to negotiate with customers, price ourselves sensibly, and look after our mental and physical well-being. That's what the next section is all about.

Managing Your Workload

Every freelance struggles with the work pipeline. It's often a "feast or famine" life, and you can swing between extremes of inhuman deadlines which you barely survive intact, to waking up to no work at all, and panicking about your survival.

We're all different, and will respond differently to these situations. Some writers absolutely thrive on the adrenaline of deadlines, and drop into an unproductive stupor when it's quiet. Others prefer a steady stream of work, and something resembling a steady salary. You need to experiment and find out what works for you. Here are some tips for keeping your work pipeline and income steady, and your output productive:

Time management

Time management is one of the hardest things for freelances to get right. Freelances are often reluctant to turn down work, but overpromising can lead to missed deadlines, and undermine your hard-won reputation. So it's vital to get a realistic handle on your available billable hours for work.

Leaving time for admin, breaks, research and marketing, it's unlikely you can work more than 5-6 billable hours a day. There are around 20 working days in a month, not allowing for public holidays. Realistically, you have 15-18 billable days to offer clients. This gives perspective. Your time is limited. When booking work, don't go over the number of available days. That way, you won't get exhausted.

Don't worry if you have to put off a client till the next month. It does no harm to let them know that you're busy. In many cases, they'll wait. At the very least, they'll respect your honesty and clarity.

"Always on" syndrome

"Always on" syndrome is the feeling of having to be available at all times. With the world moving so fast, we can feel like failures if we're not hooked up permanently online, responding immediately to client requests, emails, tweets and the news.

When I worked in a newsroom, one of the most stressful jobs was the role of copy taster, with its constant pressure of incoming newswires from around the world. Now, we've all invited that pressure into our lives and homes, in the form of social media. Many freelances even take their mobile phones on holiday.

Always-on syndrome can turn us into blue-arsed flies, feeling crazy busy and overwhelmed by all the information coming at us, but so brain-fogged that we don't get any good work out of the door.

Social media sites such as Facebook are deliberately engineered to get us hooked. They apply devious tactics such as intermittent feedback to our all-too-human brains, to pull us in. Knowing that your feelings are induced by a deliberate design mechanism can make it easier to take a step back.

Don't feel guilty about not being "always on." To be productive, I sometimes need to go dark for a while. If clients know this is your process, they'll adapt. If work gets to the level where incoming messages derail your productive output, consider hiring a virtual assistant to field calls and emails, so that you don't miss out on work opportunities.

Time visualization

As already mentioned, your time is limited, so it makes sense to become more mindful of how you use it. Some of the concepts below may help you to visualize and manage your time better:

Life diary. This is a powerful tool. Once you truly wake up to the fact that your lifespan is limited, and the next 20 years may be all you have left, your energy can suddenly snap into focus.

A year to live. If this were your last year on the planet, what choices would you make? How exercised would you get by small things, and what would you just ignore, to make space for what really matters?

Imagine your own funeral. Lurk in the imaginary aisles and listen in. Are your ambitions represented? Are you happy with what you hear? What do you need to get more fire in your belly about?

These approaches might seem a little morbid, but they're good for a sense of focus and perspective.

Perfectionism

On the face of it, perfectionism is a good quality. Copywriting can persist for years, and careful work is needed to get the best results for your clients. But don't take perfectionism too far. Spending more time than the job really warrants can mean diminishing returns. Sometimes, it means the difference between getting a good rate for the job, and getting below the minimum wage.

Learn to differentiate between job types. Know when to pull out all the stops (say, for packaging, banner ads, straplines and anything enduring), and especially anything printed on a large scale, whether large dimensions, or a big print run. Know also when a good professional job is good enough (say, product descriptions for nearly identical widgets, or meta descriptions for SEO). They may not need to be poetry-perfect.

Unless you're working for a client who pays top dollar and values every ounce of your effort, stick to your agreed two editing rounds. Write great copy, but target your best creative energy towards the kind of work that has most impact.

Time bandits

Added threats to your steely freelance resolve include other freelance friends. There's nothing better than a catch-up with colleagues, but time over coffee and chat can pass very quickly, and before you know it, you've spent a whole day and earned nothing.

Clients can also be time-thieves. Are you charging for meetings? Make sure they know your policy. You may find unnecessary check-ins suddenly stop. Beware of long "getting-to-know-you" meetings with new clients. Start-ups in particular love talking through their plans, and getting advice. Don't inadvertently become one of their free consultants.

When does a "chat" become a "consultation"? I suggest after an hour. When arranging a pre-engagement meeting, make clear you only have an hour. This puts you in control, and establishes clear expectations from the start.

Private sector workers are usually efficient with their time, but public sector workers are occasionally over-fond of meetings. With a guaranteed income at the end of the month, they're not under the same pressure to work fast and effectively, and the real cost of all the people around the table at a meeting is often staggering.

If you're paid by the hour, time is your currency. You only have one life, so pull focus, and don't indulge people who waste yours. Once you grasp this principle, any former gripes about the tyranny of agendas, systems and pressure fade away. Business practices like this are often just a way to help people to focus and conserve energy in a pressurized environment.

The worst boss in the world

The worst boss in the world might well be *you*. It's amazing how many freelances turn into awful, despotic unfeeling bosses. Watch out for any of the following bad behaviours:

❋ **Do you pay yourself properly?**
Lots of freelances don't pay themselves enough. They bust a gut for clients, put in extra hours at ridiculous times, forego days off, and still don't come away with a decent pay check. If this is you, see **Improve your Bottom Line**.

116

✳ Do you take holidays?

The freedom to take holidays when you want is part of the vision for many freelances. But the reality is often very different. Some freelances seem to view holidays as lazy and self-indulgent. Some work weekends, too. When others are off to the beach in the summer, they're still sweating away at the desk, chained to their groaning workload.

But you can't carry on running on empty. Going too long without a decent break is counter-productive. Your brain and creativity can become dull and dysfunctional without a change of scene, or some relaxed time to disengage. It's actually far more productive to take breaks and come back refreshed. Tell that to your heartless boss.

If you're one of those workaholic freelances, reframe holidays as a necessary evil to boost your productivity, and head for the hills at least twice a year. And don't take your mobile.

✳ Do you take screen breaks?

During my early journalism training, my boss insisted on screen breaks and stretching every half hour – part of their commitment to our health and well-being. Yet when I started working for myself, this habit flew out of the window.

If you're up against a deadline, it's very easy to find your eyes permanently glued to the screen. You may end up sitting for long periods in the same position, getting stiff and unfit. If you find it hard to build a screen break habit, use the Pomodoro technique, or get a fitness tracker with a "move yourself" function.

✳ Do you have insurance?

What would happen if you suddenly became ill, couldn't do your work, and had to meet mortgage payments, client commitments, and other obligations. Are you covered?

117

❂ **Do you have a pension?**
This isn't a personal finance book, so I'll leave that thunderous question echoing in the air. But when you're setting rates and charging clients, remember that you're responsible for setting yourself up to survive old age, assuming that you retire at all. If nothing else, this will encourage you to charge a sensible rate for your excellent work.

❂ **Do you put up with conditions you'd never tolerate if you were working for someone else?**
Such as an airless room, freezing temperatures, rickety chair, perilous piles of books and papers, no fire extinguisher, dangerously fizzing electric points? If so, scream at your boss to get the health and safety person in. Which is probably you. That's the multi-hatted joy of being freelance.

Managing Yourself

When you work for yourself, you're your best and only asset. It follows that you need to look after yourself. If things go wrong, you can't just trade yourself in, or get a newer model.

You're unique. And you don't have a backup. So from now on, treat yourself like an amazing piece of irreplaceable equipment. A vintage Rolls Royce or beautifully engineered steam engine. Whatever works for you.

Your brain and body are part of that same wonderful machinery, and trouble at one end affects the other. Here are some thoughts for keeping everything in good working order:

Body
Now that you know your body is irreplaceable and valuable, it's a short step to thinking of it as one of your best business assets.

118

So staying reasonably intact is a good business decision. On the operational front, this means:

- Don't get a bad back.
- Don't get RSI.
- Stay sane.

Back, shoulders, hands

Look after your back, shoulders and hands by checking out your desk ergonomics. Is your chair at the right height? Do you have a decent keyboard? Prevent RSI by stretching out and taking plenty of screen breaks. A "proper screen break" means get up, walk around, stretch your legs, get some fresh air into your lungs, and some movement into your nervous system.

Recent research has raised concern about the link between a sedentary lifestyle and all sorts of diseases. Apparently, we can't sit at our desks all day, then undo the damage with a full-on hour at the gym. Little and often is far more effective, as it keeps your circulation going and stops blood pooling and general sluggishness.

If you want to get technical about your fitness, invest in a fitness tracker such as a Fitbit. Some of them have a "reminder to move" feature which beeps if you haven't budged for the last hour. This can be an eye-opener. You may be shocked about how little you're moving during a day of work.

For other body-friendly tips, see **Sit-Stand Desk** and **DragonDictate**.

Repetitive Strain Injury (RSI)

RSI is a real danger for working writers. We're hunched all day over laptops, after all, and rarely go out to eat, play or exercise. Particularly if you're a fast touch typist, with a flickering keyboard action, you may be prone to RSI. Once RSI kicks in, it's hard to get rid of, so prevention is far better than cure. Guard against it by regularly stretching your hands, fingers, wrists and shoulders, and staying mobile.

Ergonomic chairs and the right desk height can certainly help, but the key defences are variety and mobility of posture. Keep the blood flowing to your extremities, so your nerves are always nourished. Avoid sitting in cramped positions, and be especially careful if you're writing in non-work environments such as cafés, or at home on the kitchen table. These surfaces are usually higher than the ideal height for keyboard work.

If you use a lot of repetitive phrases, set up macros. This can be particularly useful for clients with technical terminology.

The mouse is another common culprit in RSI, as it encourages an unnatural hovering hand position with no wrist support. Wherever possible, use keyboard shortcuts rather than the mouse. At the very least, learn how to bold, italicize, highlight, cut, copy and paste using the keyboard. If you're looking for a real game-changer, consider **DragonDictate** dictation software.

Eyes

At the computer, our eyes tend to focus on a very narrow, close-up range. But your eyes are controlled by muscles, just like the rest of your body, and need to be exercised. During screen breaks, shut your eyes, and give them a change of focal length by going outside and focusing on the horizon.

Fresh air is helpful, too. Eyes get dry after hours of screen-staring. Drink plenty of liquids, ideally water. Added bonus: going to the toilet a lot means you get up and stretch your legs.

Brain

For copywriters, your brain is even more valuable and irreplaceable than your body. Think of it as a priceless Stradivarius, or finely tuned antique Swiss watch.

Brains use a surprising amount of energy when working at full capacity. Take this into account, and don't overdo it. It's very easy as a freelance to get so booked up on client work that you never get away on holiday. This is not only dispiriting and exhausting. It's also counter-productive, and bad business. A tired brain takes twice as long to do jobs.

Make sure you get holidays, weekends and time to regenerate in between bursts of full-on work. Your neurons will thank you.

Variety & stimulation

Sometimes, freelance writers work so hard that they end up running on empty creatively. We can't keep giving out, producing, and writing, without also spending time renewing ourselves, and finding stimulus and interest. Make sure you set aside time for new and stimulating experiences, even if it's just trying a different café, walking a different route, going into a new shop or gallery.

If you're up against it and notice diminishing returns setting in, don't just take a break. Step away, and do something completely different. Jolt your brain into a different headspace to fire things up again.

Luckily, clients are an ever-fascinating source of inspiration and information. Ring one up, and drop around for a coffee. You may even bring some new work in.

Isolation

Writers spend a lot of time on their own. Most enjoy their own company, so you might think this isn't a problem. But over time, isolation can start to affect people in strange ways.

A lack of social interaction, even if you're an introvert and actually prefer it, can lead to depression. It's easy to forget that in addition to a regular pay check, regular employment provides structure, social context, status and stimulus. To a great extent, it also contributes to your identity. Without these things, people can sometimes struggle, especially after the novelty of freedom has worn off.

A copywriter needs to build new working relationships and find colleagues to exchange with – not just for business, but also for interaction, friendship and social structure. That's one of the reasons why businesses like to network.

Focus & flow

Copywriting productivity is directly linked to your ability to focus for long periods. This capacity is highly individual, but it's amazing how many creative writers struggle with distraction, and find writing mentally exhausting.

Most journalists, on the other hand, can write and edit for hours at a stretch. This is partly to do with the nature of the writing. With journalism, you're often weaving known facts together, and using repetitive phrasing, whereas creative writers often write to explore and discover, without knowing the territory in advance.

Copywriting is somewhere in between. It's far easier to get into a flow state if you know your material and audience really well. Knowing the word length and space you're writing to helps, too.

Many writers swear by the "Pomodoro" technique of 25-minute work bursts, followed by five-minute breaks. When I'm feeling resistance, I set a timer and do pomodoros.

 Workwise:

If you're sensitive to sound, you don't need fancy noise-cancelling headphones to minimize distractions. Just get a pair of industrial ear defenders from any DIY supplier. They're inexpensive and cut out most sound. They're ideal on long journeys. Folding ones take up less space.

Managing Clients

It's hard to generalize here. Clients are all very different. But you may be surprised to learn how many prefer *you* to take control. Many clients haven't dealt with copywriters before, and may not have a clue about how the process works. Or they may read up on "how to manage copywriters," and set unhelpful rules, without really understanding what you can do for them. So be prepared to step in and lead the conversation and process, manage the project and, if necessary, also the client.

Setting boundaries

Get off on a clear footing by setting boundaries. Brief the client on your process, including Terms and Conditions. Negotiate and agree payment and deadlines. Make sure the client understands when they're paying for your time. After an introductory meeting, your time no no longer comes free – you're on the clock. This will help them to be efficient and decisive, and speed up the work.

Don't make a habit of replying instantly to client phone calls and emails. This may seem counter-intuitive, but quick responses can encourage unrealistic expectations. Clients may start ringing you about tiny matters, or sending jobs with impossible deadlines, expecting you to drop everything.

Ask clients to send queries by email. This not only helps you to manage your time better, but also gives you a written record of your interaction. Ideally, ask your client to batch several queries together. This will save you time, and encourage them to think things through before sending.

Clients who don't know they need you

The world is full of websites and print promotions with terrible copy. Great! An endless supply of businesses needing your services, right? Sadly, it doesn't work like that. Many businesses don't know they need a copywriter. They may not even know copywriters exist.

It's tempting to approach businesses with a poor website, offer to help, and try to win them as a client. Be careful here. It's fine to drop a leaflet or a quick email, to make them aware of your services. But don't spend any more time than that. Why? Because if someone doesn't know they need help, you'll need to convince them. Educating clients about copywriting, and the value of your services, takes time. And they still may not appreciate your services, or want to pay the going rate.

By far the best clients are the ones that come to you, ideally through word-of-mouth, because they heard you speak at a workshop, or saw your work for another client. With these clients, you don't need to sell, or explain what your services can do.

They're already on side, prepared to pay the going rate, and likely to appreciate your work.

Rather than spending time on educating individual clients, consider:

- giving a talk at your local business networking club
- writing a blog
- preparing a handout or leaflet
- making a video.

Then signpost casual inquirers to this information, with an invitation to call you if they're interested in taking things further.

Perfectionist clients

Perfectionism cuts two ways. Some perfectionist clients are great. They know what they want. They may have exceptionally high standards that push you hard. They may enjoy the to-and-fro of the creative process, and be creative and visually aware themselves. Clients like this can help you and graphic or web design colleagues to achieve exceptional results for their business, and an ideal calling card for your future work. If you do a sterling job for an exacting client, they'll be your best advocates, and you'll get good word of mouth.

But perfectionists can also go in a different direction entirely. Some clients know exactly what they *don't* want, but can't explain what they *do* want. They may insist on micro-managing every tiny detail, but never be happy with the result. They may be indecisive, or influenced by managers, friends and spouses. A client like this may have control issues, and never be satisfied. This is an inefficient way of working, and can make you feel insecure.

Again, clear expectations from the start will help to nip this situation in the bud. Get what the client wants in writing, and follow it to the letter, including the number of revision drafts. Keep records, and don't waste time trying to satisfy impossible demands.

124

Assert your worth

Some clients are willing to pay for good photography, design skills, and four-colour printing for a glossy brochure, yet balk at written content. Be cautious about clients that don't care about the copy, or see it just as "filler." I've even had a client say "nobody reads it anyway." Nowadays, I'd walk away. A client like this isn't going to value your work, or the time you spend. It may also be (as in this case) that you're dealing with someone with mild dyslexia, who is uncomfortable around words.

Get a sense of what others in the team are being paid, and make sure you're on the same level. With website jobs, learn to argue the case for skilled copywriting. Often clients who don't appreciate copywriting understand the need for SEO and being found on the web.

Be on guard

There are charlatans in business, as in any walk of life. Most difficulties arise around payment. Occasionally, people in business can be unscrupulous and "try it on." However, it's unlikely you'll encounter a classic moustache-twirling felon. A far more likely scenario is sliding into a relationship, having a couple of exploratory meetings, and finding yourself doing some work, without clarity about the process, or commitments on either side. Note that just because someone is on the doorstep, or referred by someone you know, doesn't mean they're intrinsically reliable. Always be friendly, open and helpful, but protect yourself with a clear process and boundaries.

Managing Collaboration

As a copywriter, you'll often work with collaborators, including graphic and web designers. Mostly, jobs will be led by the client or the designer, and you'll be in a sub-contracting role. In this case, you'll probably bill your own services separately. Usually, I send my final invoice for copy as soon as I've supplied the signed-off draft. It may be a long time before the project is live or completed, so don't wait till then.

When working on a job for a bigger client, clarify the lines of communication. Sometimes responsibilities can get blurred when several people are involved. The habit of copying everyone in on every email can mean no one thinks they're responsible, and jobs can fall between the cracks. It's a good idea to agree a point of contact, so that you're only answerable to one person. Keep emails, so that you have a record of each stage.

This makes collaboration sound harder than it is. Most jobs are straightforward, but bear in mind that you're often dealing with people and situations in flux. A certain amount of give-and-take and flexible thinking is often needed.

A Creative's Guide to Business

The world of business is enormous, and it can be hard to know where to start. If you're like me, looking at the newspaper's business pages makes you glaze over. Terms like "global market," "profit margin" and "SME" may send shivers down your spine.

The good news is you don't need to know about big business, and a lack of business training doesn't mean you can't write copy. The glossary in this book will give you most of the concepts you need to start with. Once you find clients, you'll swot up on their market, competitors and trade magazines, to learn about their sector and product-specific vocabulary and issues.

Business people don't necessarily have qualifications in business, either. Many simply dive in and learn on the job. So don't worry about your lack of business background. You'll learn through experience. And as a consumer exposed to marketing techniques, with a writer's understanding of empathy and connection, you're already more expert than you think. Many of the basic skills of business are common sense.

Business People in Brief

Ask a bunch of creative writers about the connotations of the word "business," and you may get lots of sharp suits, sharp practices, and people shouting "taxi!" But don't confuse huge corporations, retail giants and Fortune 500 companies with the businesses you may be writing for.

The world of business is extremely varied, covering everyone from part-time home-based craft workers, to mighty manufacturing empires building the roads we drive on, and the hospitals we're born and die in. So you'll find all kinds of people involved, including some you know.

By far the biggest market for freelance copywriting is small and medium enterprises, or SMEs. With this kind of company, you're mostly dealing with business owners, not employees, and they've often started up on their own. This tells you a lot about the kind of people you're dealing with.

Why do people start a business?

To earn a living. To be independent. Because they were hopeless at everything else at school. Because they have a strong streak of individualism, drive and creativity. Because they're big dreamers. Because they want freedom – financial freedom, and freedom from overbearing bosses they don't agree with.

So, in some ways, they're much like writers and artists. Except that business owners have saddled themselves with employees, premises, wage bills, red tape and taxes, in pursuit of their passion.

Business owners are highly driven and can be impatient. There's a lot at stake, and the buck stops with them. Be prepared to share your client's enthusiasm about their dream, and step into their shoes. Be prepared also to step back, and not be swept up so much that you're blind to the realities. Imagine a ship trying to stay afloat in unpredictable waters. You may be their great hope. Your copy is going to magically get the orders surging in. No pressure!

Types of Business

Businesses can be categorized in different ways, according to scale, sector, market, and other features. Awareness of these categories is useful for understanding clients' businesses, and can also help you understand your own place in the market. Here are some common business categorizations used by enterprise bodies, with some notes relevant to copywriting.

Size of business

Businesses can be categorized by size. Different countries use slightly different definitions. Broadly speaking, they are:

Large companies

More than 250 employees.

Larger companies often have in-house marketing teams, or use agencies. Unless you're a full-time career freelance copywriter, this probably won't be your main source of clients.

Small or medium enterprises (SMEs)

10-250 employees, sometimes divided into small (10-50) and medium (50-250).
This is a huge category. The vast majority of businesses are SMEs, and small businesses aren't necessarily all that small. In most countries, they're the backbone of the economy, making up by far the majority (well over 90%) of all companies.

At the mid-to-high end of the scale, SMEs are significant employers in their local economy, and need to work hard and effectively to win enough sales to sustain those jobs. As a freelance copywriter, this is likely to be your main market.

Micro-businesses

Businesses with fewer than 10 employees.
These include many:

- trades, professions and freelancers
- independent shops with no ambitions to expand
- family-run tourism and hospitality businesses.

Aspirational micro-businesses with a marketing budget can be a good source of clients.

It's worth noting that traditionally, enterprise bodies have concentrated on SMEs, with micro-businesses taking a back seat. However, micro-businesses are increasingly being acknowledged as a vital part of the economy, particularly in rural areas.

Business life span

As already mentioned, businesses have a life span, just like those larva-pupa-butterflies in TV documentaries.

Businesses are born, mature and grow. They have teething troubles and growing pains. Sometimes they also die and self-destruct in spectacular fashion. It's helpful to know what stage of the lifecycle your client's business is at, as this will influence what they need from a copywriter.

For most purposes, the stages you need to know about are start-up and growth.

Start-up

Start-ups range from tiny bootstrap businesses to high-growth start-ups with enterprise funding. The business owners may be inexperienced, and you'll be helping them to break new ground and articulate their idea. If the company and its products inspire you, it's wonderful to be in on the start, and know you played a part. If everything goes well, you may become a regular part of their success story.

But be careful: working with start-ups is a big responsibility, and not every new business owner is a natural entrepreneur. Your input can help to make or break the business's success.

New business owners often need guidance, and are keen to talk to people who can help, so you may find them needing more input than you expected. Your client may not have a copywriting brief, marketing plan, or even a crystal-clear idea of their target customer. If this happens, you may need to step in and provide a framework for your copywriting services.

Established business

Established businesses have survived the teething pains of start-up, and are operating comfortably in their niche. They may need to refresh their image, or outrun new competition. These businesses have typically done some marketing before, and may already have a brand, logos, a marketing plan and print promotions. If so, you can draw on their previous experience, and may not need to work from scratch.

Growth business

Some businesses don't plan to grow, and that's fine. As long as they continue to be viable, they're happy not to expand. A growth business, on the other hand, has a mindset geared towards expansion. This may be built in from the start, or evolve naturally over time.

A growth business will typically draw on copywriting services as part of a marketing strategy, often when it's trying to reposition itself, or embrace a new direction.

A business that identifies itself as a growth business is likely to be engaging with enterprise bodies for grants and support. This means it will usually have a business and marketing plan, and should be able to brief you effectively.

Products, services

Businesses can be divided into whether they sell products or services. Some companies do both: a training company that runs workshops and sells online courses, for example, or a fridge retailer that also provides a repair service.

Companies selling products typically have larger retail websites with lots of product descriptions and strong visuals. Copywriters working for this kind of company sometimes team up with an SEO specialist to target particular market niches. Short form copy is the norm here.

Retail websites typically have a few main pages, lots of product descriptions, and sometimes a blog. It's common for retailers to ask for copy just for the main pages, and supply product descriptions themselves, as it would be too costly to hire a copywriter for these. Sometimes, you may be asked to do an SEO makeover or proofreading job on product descriptions.

Companies selling services typically have fewer website pages, and may need longer form copy. Since services are more abstract and harder to depict, case studies can be useful. The most complex service can come to life when it's attached to a story and person.

B2B, B2C

Business to business (B2B) refers to companies that sell to trade, ie to other businesses. Things that businesses may need include insurance, retail display units, components, machine tools... and copywriting. So, as a copywriter, you're a provider of B2B services.

To complicate matters, your clients may be B2B or B2C (business to consumer – ie selling direct to the public). So depending on your client's target market, your copywriting jobs will also divide into B2B and B2C.

Till now, you as a consumer have probably been exposed mainly to B2C copy – the ads and emails trying to sell you clothes, cars and chocolate. But B2B is an important area of copywriting. Some copywriters choose to specialize in B2B work.

B2B copywriting has very different demands. It rarely uses hard sell, and headline-grabbing conceptual content. People in business know the ropes, and are often immune to showy tactics. B2B marketing typically focuses on clear value propositions, practical benefits, evidence, and straight talking. Once again, case studies are useful here.

Industrial estates can be a good starting-point for finding B2B clients. Businesses in industrial estates typically aren't customer-facing. Do some research, check out the company websites, and get a sense of their size. The visual impact and size of the site will tell you something about their market, and whether they have a marketing budget.

Public sector & charities

Public and charity sector clients can be rewarding to work for, if you can find a way in. If you've worked in these sectors before, you may have contacts who can field you smaller jobs.

However, at least in the UK, public sector work above a certain value needs to go through the "procurement" system of competitive tender. Some procurement contracts are even open to international suppliers, so the process can be extremely competitive. To submit a tender, suppliers need to register on the public procurement website, and go through a rigorous process.

Small businesses typically aren't geared up for the level of administration and time investment involved in this, so the procurement process favours larger companies with greater resources. Larger suppliers are also likelier to have the well-established procedures and clear accountability favoured by the public sector.

As a freelance copywriter, you may struggle to get public sector work through the procurement process. If you want to pursue this market, consider forming a collective with other creative services, such as web and graphic design. Once you've won one public procurement contract, the door will open more easily to others.

Charities and community interest companies (CICs) may also need freelance copywriting services, though they may not have a big budget. If you have experience and contacts in this area, it may be a good source of work. Note that non-profits have different values and may not see themselves as businesses, so be prepared to research their different terminology.

Online, offline

These days, the boundaries between online and offline businesses are blurred. Most high-street traders also sell online. Many manufacturers now also have online shops and sell direct to customers. Sometimes, they compete with their own resellers and distributors, and want you to write sales copy without affecting these derivative businesses – impossible! If this happens, just do your normal job, but make the client aware of what they're asking.

133

Value chain

Businesses can be categorized by their position in the "value chain." They may be involved in processing raw materials, manufacturing, assembly, installation or distribution. Or they may be in wholesale, reselling, disposal, marketing, sales, or services.

Businesses can be built around many stages of the process of bringing products to consumers. Very few are primary producers who sell direct to customers. Understanding where your clients fit into the value chain helps to shed light on their work processes, market and customer relationships.

Finding Clients

By now, you know that SMEs are a good potential market for copywriting services. They make up 90%+ of all businesses, so that's a wide range of people who may need your words. You should be able to find companies aligned to your values, interests, and skills. The next step is to reach out to them.

If you're starting from scratch, it may be reassuring to know you don't need to target every business in the neighbourhood, send out mass mailshots, or do cold calling. I built my business without doing any of these things.

It's best to narrow your focus, to find companies where you have most chance of finding copywriting clients. At the same time, ply friends and ex-colleagues with business cards, to spread the word among their networks.

Client companies

In the world of copywriting, not all companies are created equal. Even if they're successful, and making a valuable contribution to their communities, they still might not be the right fit for your services.

For a start, very small businesses may not have the budget to hire you. Or they may be happy with how things are, enjoying great word of mouth and a full work pipeline. They may not need to do any marketing, and a sudden rush of customers might even topple the business. If they reject your offer to transform their underperforming website copy, this may be why.

Other businesses may have in-house staff who enjoy writing their brochures. The business owner might not have the verbal skills to appreciate what copywriting can do, or want to pay the going rate. They may not even know that copywriting exists.

The ideal client knows they can't write copy, and need your help. They understand that it's a specialist skill, calling for considerable knowledge and training, and are prepared to pay a good rate. Finding these clients will take some work. But once you find the first few, they'll start to spread the word for you.

SME sweet spot

The sweet spot for building your client list is SMEs who aren't yet big enough to have their own marketing provision. Or else they have a marketing officer who isn't skilled with words, and is honest enough to admit it (a rare beast).

The advantage of this scale of company is that they're likely to have an ongoing need for copywriting. If you do a good job, they may come back to you, and you'll have the beginnings of a work pipeline that doesn't require marketing effort. They're also more likely than smaller companies to understand why copywriting is important, and pay the going rate.

Bigger corporates and organizations typically already have an in-house marketing team, or contract their marketing to creative agencies. Culturally, they're more likely to work with bigger companies themselves, so you may be less likely to gain a foothold as a sole trader.

But if you have a special "in" – personal connection, or previous experience – make them your first port of call as a freelance. You could find yourself working as an external contractor, and called on for regular projects.

Sole traders may include some of your nearest and dearest friends, but they may not be a lucrative source of ongoing income.

Good ones are so booked out that they don't need to do any marketing. They may need a website and a couple of leaflets, but little more, and typically don't bring much repeat work.

Since copywriting is frontloaded in terms of research and relationship-building, you're ideally looking for work that won't just be a one-off. That means clients who'll bring repeat business, making the time invested in researching their company and sector well worth it.

Some sole traders, such as graphic designers and accountants, are B2B suppliers, and connect with a wide range of businesses. They may be a better fit for you, as they may bring clients your way.

Sectors

Copywriters with a technical specialism such as IT or engineering who are good general communicators can find their skills in high demand. Being able to bridge the gap between technical and non-technical products and services can give you a valuable USP.

Mature industries such as farming, finance and accountancy can be slow to change. By their nature, they're risk averse, so they're unlikely to be looking for a wacky campaign. They may even tone down your friendly, accessible style, to make it more formal and reserved. It may be that, as an industry built on trust, they don't want to give the impression of being casual.

If dealing with a company whose technical specialism you know nothing about, it can sometimes be inefficient to research and try to understand everything. Consider offering editing, proofing or an SEO makeover of their existing copy instead.

The Job of Writing

Copywriting has changed massively in the past few years, and different kinds of work keep emerging. Most writing for business used to be print work; now the emphasis has shifted to web.

Though most copywriters do both, it's important to recognize that they draw on different skills and styles. Some copywriters no longer work for print at all, preferring to specialize in SEO copy, which calls for strong digital skills.

The emphasis on "content" in the digital world has also changed how writing skills are perceived and marketed – something to be aware of when reaching out to client businesses.

Print and web writing also differ in the kinds of team members you'll collaborate with. Print writing partners are usually graphic designers, while web writing partners may be web designers or SEO specialists.

Here's a breakdown of the main differences and challenges:

Writing for Print

Despite the rise of digital marketing, print is still important. One of the reasons is the longevity of print. It's easy to close a website and forget it – out of sight, out of mind. But a brochure or leaflet is harder to discard. Many online retailers, particularly in fashion and lifestyle, still invest in print catalogues. Their book-like form makes them attractive – something for customers to hang onto, and return to.

Colour printing is also getting cheaper, thanks to digital technology opening up small print runs and print on demand. This puts print material within the reach of even tiny businesses. So print is here to stay.

What's different about print?

The longevity and prestige of print has implications for copywriters. Clearly, whether you're writing for print or web, perfect spelling and grammar are vital. But with print, your creation may stay around for a long time. I found one tourism leaflet I wrote still being used ten years later, even though some of the places it mentioned had closed.

Particularly for print jobs, if you can, it's a good idea to work closely with the designer, respecting their process and responding to their drafts. The client will get a far better result, and you'll have a great portfolio piece which will do good business for you.

 Workwise:

I was asked to write 300 words for a DL trifold leaflet. After checking with the designer and client, we cut it to 150, and fit everything in beautifully. At the last minute, the client added QR codes and several logos. Instead of contacting the copywriter for a rewrite, the designer reduced the font size, making it nearly impossible to read. Make sure you see the final proofs of any print job!

Writing process for print

Websites have infinite capacity, so it can be hard to know how much copy to write. Print materials have limited space, which makes life much easier. If you're a journalist, you'll be used to supplying the right word count for a specific print space. This approach is helpful for copywriting, too. When doing a print job, get in touch with the designer to find out how many words they need. They may even already have started the design, and send you a mock-up. With word counts, take a steer from the designer, not the client. The client may be guessing.

Always ask to see proofs. You'll be amazed at how much your copy can change in others' hands, and so many mistakes creep in at the last minute. Hyphenation and line run-ons are another last-minute problem area, especially with short copy such as ads and product labels. A savvy copywriter can solve these issues at the proofing stage. This extra layer of polish and flow can make all the difference to the overall impact, and the designer and client will appreciate your care and professionalism.

Small print runs

The traditional process for print publication is litho, which is great for high quality print copy and high volume runs. However, digital print has improved greatly, to the point where the quality difference is no longer so obvious. It's now possible to print small runs far more economically, which is great for small businesses who typically may not see print as a good investment. PDF case studies can also be emailed around, posted on your website, printed out on good quality paper as takeaways, and updated when circumstances change. So for a small upfront investment, small businesses can get a lot of value.

Consistency

At the start of each job, note any recurring terminology, and clarify how the client wants it to be styled. For example, do they prefer capital letters for "board of management"? Do they refer to their audience as "users," "service users," "clients," or "customers"? This will save work later.

For general consistency, I use the conventions in the *Oxford English Dictionary*, along with the *Oxford University Style Guide*, which provides a modern, uncluttered layout. It's a good idea to stick to a particular style guide, and suggest your preference to the client and designer. It saves arguments and time.

Writing for the Web

Copywriting for the web calls for the same broad writing skills as writing for print, as well as some extra skills that may be new to you. With web writing, you're writing not just for the target reader, but also to boost search engine rankings. Copywriters specialising in writing for the web call themselves "SEO copywriters" or "SEO content writers."

If you're technically and analytically minded, you may want to consider specializing in SEO, and go on to learn about Google Analytics and digital marketing. Most SEO specialists aren't trained writers with the skills to disguise SEO tactics, so this could give you a lucrative niche.

Search engines are evolving all the time, so SEO tactics that work one month may not work the next. Companies sometimes put their efforts behind a specific SEO strategy, only to find their sites taking a big dive in search rankings, when Google changes its algorithms. The only consistently powerful strategy is fresh, relevant, well-written content that people want to read. This is good news for writers.

People and pixels

When people started out writing for the web, the new platform was treated as a version of a book or newspaper, and writers approached it in a similar way. But as we learn more about how people read and retain information on the web, different writing styles are evolving. This evolution is also affected by the ever-shrinking size of reading devices such as tablets and smartphones. Another important consideration is that people reading on the web are often looking for information, usually as quickly as possible.

So even setting aside SEO considerations, web copy still has different features to print copy, including:

- ❀ shorter sentences, for easier flow on small devices
- ❀ headers, bullet points and paragraphs to break up the text
- ❀ hyperlinks
- ❀ non-linear flow, with more jumping around for the reader.

Distracting ads and animations also make it much harder to retain a reader's attention, so reading is experienced as less immersive than in print. This means writers need to cut to the chase, and avoid introductory scene-setting. Overall, writing for the web uses all your usual strategies, but with even greater emphasis on clarity and brevity.

SEO copy

SEO stands for "search engine optimization." SEO copy is the art of writing content that is ranked high by search engines. In the early days of the web, this was something of a dark art. Shrewd web developers and writers could game the system by loading the copy with search terms – a process known as "keyword stuffing." If you were marketing a disposable widget, the words "disposable widget" had to appear as many times as possible within the text. This led to shouty, unnatural web copy with a high keyword density.

This kind of content approach is sometimes called "black hat," from the "good guy" and "bad guy" hats worn in westerns. Other black hat practices include using other companies' brand names in your keywords, or adding backlinks to your own site on competitors' blogs. Thankfully, Google and other search engines now penalize these practices, in their quest to "introduce good quality content to the reader who wants it."

Search engines in brief

A complete SEO copywriting primer is a book in itself, but the good news is that a few basic principles will get you a long way. Search engine-friendly writing means writing for two different conceptual spaces:

Firstly, the **body content**. This is the copy on the actual webpages and blogs which is clearly visible on the web, to both people and search bots.

Secondly, the **structural content**. This is the behind-the-scenes text that helps search engines. It includes meta descriptions, tags, headlines, titles and other structural elements of a site. Some of these are invisible to people, and planted solely for search bots.

These structural elements are a code that helps the bots to do their work. Some, such as meta descriptions and page titles, can be seen when you do a web search. Others, such as tags, can only be seen by viewing the source code.

 Workwise:
To see the inner workings of any web page, right-click on it, and choose "view source." This stream of apparent gobbledygook is the hidden language of websites, and includes any written content.

It's worth looking at the source code to understand an important fundamental: Search engines need words.

In amongst all the code and numbers, bots are actually truffle-hunting the best words relevant to each search. You don't need to write code, but if you can write the basic bot-friendly elements, you're on your way to being an SEO copywriter.

Meta descriptions

Meta descriptions are the two-line elements ("snippets") of text that appear in search results. If you haven't inspected them before, take a look now, by opening your browser and doing a search.

Meta descriptions are a mini taster for the web page. They help visitors to decide whether to click on the site – essentially a free advertising space – so they need to be specially written. If you spot a meta description filled with incoherent text, it's because the bots didn't find a pre-written snippet, and used whatever was to hand.

An SEO copywriter will supply separate meta descriptions for each page. This is typically a customer-friendly sentence or two, of no more than 140 characters.

URLs

URLs are the web address at the top of every website page. Any words they contain need to be carefully considered from a marketing and keyword point of view.

This isn't really a copywriter's job. It's an SEO job. Ideally, your client should either hire an SEO expert, or do their own research. However, some awareness of SEO considerations can help you give a valuable steer to clients.

For example, a URL that includes "cheap-flights" is likely to get more hits than one with "low-cost-flights," simply because it's a more intuitive, easily typed search term. You can help clients and web designers to make better choices by making sure the URLs include words customers might use in search. These may not be the words most used by companies, who are often steeped in expert vocabulary.

If you're working with an SEO specialist, they should supply you with a list of site URLs containing keywords agreed with the client. If not, check in with the website designer, for a clear understanding of the site map and intended URLs.

Content

"Content" is a rather maligned term amongst writers. It conjures up the unfortunate image of bottomless digital vats waiting for "stuff" to be poured into them, whatever the quality. However, it's really just a matter of terminology. People searching the internet are looking for something – mostly information and entertainment. "Content" is whatever meets their needs.

Content farms deserve special mention because some writers have been lured into writing for them for ridiculously low pay. Don't go there! This activity is at the low end of the internet market, highly exploitative, and needn't concern you. Mass-produced content is increasingly filtered out by search engines, in any case.

Be aware, however, that you may be asked to write "SEO content," as SEO specialists widely use this terminology. If you work with an SEO specialist, they'll usually provide the URL, some keywords, and the target audience, and you then write to that brief. The trick is writing within these tight parameters in an engaging way that hides any clunky SEO techniques.

If you can write creatively to order, you may find SEO specialists knocking at your door. Or, even better, acquire those skills yourself. SEO specialists are often paid a monthly retainer, so it can be lucrative and regular work.

SEO is the Wild West of marketing. The territory is constantly shifting, and you need to be prepared to keep up with training, algorithms and future developments such as the "semantic web." If this sounds exciting rather than terrifying, it may be for you.

Spinning

"Spinning" is an example of SEO gone very wrong. It refers to the practice of slightly rewriting copy to avoid search engine penalties for repetition or plagiarism. The rewriting is done by software which acts like a word-laundry, rejigging the text and substituting synonyms to make it look new. If you dare, do a search for "article spinning." If this concept is new to you, your writer soul will probably need time to recover. The good news is, black hat practices such as this are heavily penalized by search engines. Even sophisticated plagiarism can now be picked up by software.

Business blogging

Blogging is another area where copywriters can help businesses. Often, people don't have the time to write their own blogs on a regular basis. Many new sites start off with great enthusiasm with two or three blogs, then peter out. You can help here, by providing business owners with a straightforward solution. If you do this well, it can become a regular source of income.

Some copywriters offer to "content manage" client sites. This means offering an end-to-end service, including posting the blog and sometimes images on the client's websites. To make this more economical for clients, offer to batch up items and do several at once, saving time on both sides.

Blogs tend to come in two main flavours: short news items to be turned around quickly, and longer feature-style items aimed at boosting SEO. If you take on blogging work, put a date in the diary to speak to the client once a month, get their ideas and ask questions (new staff, new products?) to see if there's anything they've missed.

Once you get to know clients, they may give you access to their site logons, so that you can post directly to the site, saving them time. Just be careful here – don't do it unless you're very confident of your CMS skills. If you do go ahead, ask your client to sign a disclaimer. You don't want to be liable if something goes wrong with their site.

Short blogs aren't a lucrative source of income, but a blogging specialism could develop into a work pipeline, if you find a large number of clients.

Website endgame

Websites are prone to end-of-project expansion, with extra requests arising as the deadline approaches, or when the development site goes up. Potential problems to watch out for include click-through buttons and calls to action. These are often added in by the web designer, using a standard text which may be at odds with the tone of the website.

Before the site goes live, check it through. Open a Word document to collect feedback notes. If you spot a mistake, grab the URL of the page, copy the problem text, and highlight the change. **(CTRL + ALT + H)**

Web developers love this, because it allows them to go straight to the page, find the change and sort it, with minimum fuss. Most importantly, it means the resulting site is a good reflection of you and the quality of your work. There's nothing worse than doing a great copywriting job, visiting the live site, and finding a spelling howler in a big button on the homepage.

Rough drafts on the web

Sometimes website clients ask for rough draft copy to be posted on the development site "to get a look at it," thinking they can sort it later. It's best to strongly discourage this, for several reasons.

Firstly, it's expensive. The draft copy will need to be edited in the CMS by the developer, and your client will pay a fortune for tweaks that would take you half the time. Secondly, it encourages clients to be indecisive, which prolongs the process for you and the developer.

Fiddling with draft copy within the CMS is a bad idea also for technical reasons. Text and font changes, hyperlinks, styles, image resizing... these tweaks can all affect the code behind the scenes. The text can look fine in the CMS, but may contain legacy code, and perform badly in some browsers.

If you're uploading copy to a site, get into the habit of "cleaning" it first, particularly if you've lifted it from Microsoft Word. Word often includes invisible extra formating which can play havoc with browsers.

To clean copy, open Notepad (part of Microsoft Office), paste in the copy, then recopy it **(CTRL + A, CTRL + C)**, and paste it into the website CMS **(CTRL + V)**. This simple copy-and-paste process strips out any extra coding, leaving you with pristine text for dropping into the website.

Copywriting Job Types

Copywriting is a broad church, and businesses come in infinite varieties. As a copywriter for SMEs, you need to be a flexible problem solver, able to turn your hand to many different kinds of work, whether websites, newsletters, blogs, banners, brochures, straplines, case studies, or presentations. The only way to really learn is to study examples, dive in, practise, and absorb what you can from each experience. While there are no typical jobs or clients, here are some thoughts on forms you may be less familiar with:

Straplines

A strapline is a short phrase of only a few words that captures a business's product and personality, and often sits under the company logo. In an ideal world, a company's strapline is developed early on, as part of the branding process. In practice, particularly with start-ups, there may be a skimpy branding process at best, and you may be asked to come up with something very late in the day. The client is essentially asking you to provide a quick, no-budget version of a normally expensive service.

If this happens, point out that straplines need careful consideration. They're crucial to the company's identity, and will appear everywhere, for years: in print, on the web, on exhibition stands, and on van liveries. They need a long shelf life. Charge by the hour, and come up with several variations. The process of working through different options will help the client to clarify their thoughts.

Packaging and labels

Product packaging comes with certain regulatory requirements, and your client needs to know these. Regulations are particularly stringent in the case of food, and products destined for export. Food ingredients need to be listed in a particular order, and washing and care instructions need to be expressed in a particular way. Products may even need a disclaimer, or other elements with legal implications. This isn't your job, but do check your client has researched this, and provides the correct wording, especially if you're dealing with a start-up.

For jobs like this, work closely with the graphic designer. Packaging and labels are like tiny poems (at least in layout terms),

147

so be prepared to suggest tweaks for hyphenation, justification, line endings, and word swops or additions to make the space work well for the eye. It's also easy to miss out items such as web addresses and phone numbers. Check against similar products, and use a checklist.

Case studies

A case study is a form of "soft" marketing which sells the client's business indirectly. Typically, it describes how the company solved a particular customer problem, and will include quotes from the happy customer. For example, a construction company might commission a case study to showcase a house build, explaining the specification and challenges of the build project, supported by testimony from the homeowners.

Case studies are good for copywriters, as they use similar techniques to journalism, and are long form pieces of work. Usually, you'll interview the client's customer, to get their authentic viewpoint, quotes and colour, and bring the case study to life.

It's best if clients choose a case study subject that aligns well with their marketing strategy and SEO goals, perhaps illustrating a specific business strand or type of client. The chosen customer needs to be positive about the company, and happy to be interviewed, and have their comments published on the internet. Case studies can be anonymized if the customer or topic demands it. Clarify the planned use, publication and confidentiality with the customer in advance.

PART IV

Grow Your Business

For most freelance writers, being a sole trader is enough. If you've established a good work pipeline, manageable systems, and a decent income, this may be all you need. There will come times, however, when work gets too much, or you get fed up with the feast-famine cycle, and start wondering about other options.

This section looks at business and income growth as they relate to freelances, and the different ways freelances can maximize the value of their time.

Your limited time

For sole traders, the main limitation on earning more income is your time. If you're running yourself ragged and not making a good living, first look closely at how you're spending your time.

Are you wasting it on unimportant activities? Are you working enough billable hours? Are you charging enough? Are you constantly working with new clients, rather than getting repeat work from existing ones? All these factors influence what you can earn from the limited hours in your day. Small tweaks to each of them can have a big impact.

Improve your bottom line

Ideally, you want to make decent money from your hard work and creativity. Breaking it down, there are really only a few ways to improve your bottom line:

- work longer hours (time)
- work harder (intensity)
- work smarter (efficiency)
- cut costs
- charge more
- get more sales.

The first three are about process, and the second three about money. Each of these is a point of leverage where adjustments can be made to your business. So let's look at these in turn:

Work longer hours (time)

Are you already putting in a decent day's work? Or are you kidding yourself? Consider whether you:

- monitor your working hours
- dive straight into billable work, or knock off minor admin jobs first
- surf the internet/answer emails first thing, or work on client jobs.

If you're only working three billable hours a day, then increase those hours.

Of course, it's also possible you have the opposite problem: working all day, evenings and weekends, not taking holidays, and leaving no time to recharge. See **Managing Your Workload** for suggestions.

Work harder (intensity)

If you're already working a lot of hours, are they truly productive? Are you really focused? When you work on your own, it's easy to drift. Deadlines can seem less urgent. The lack of accountability means it's easier to get distracted, and there are no colleagues around to gee each other along when one of you has less energy.

As well as monitoring billable hours, work out how you're spending non-billable time. Common time wasters include phone calls, web surfing, travel and meetings. The cost of four people around a table at a meeting can be eye-watering. What do you have to show for it? Would the energy of meetings and travel be more productively spent on writing?

Don't forget also that full-on, intense work needs to be counterbalanced with breaks, otherwise fatigue and diminishing returns can set in. Step away from the keyboard entirely at regular intervals. You'll refresh your brain, jog your neurons, and gain a new perspective on tricky problems. Some writers swear by the Pomodoro technique of 25-minute work bursts, followed by a five-minute break.

Work smarter (efficiency)

Are you doing lots of short, bitty work, or bigger, meatier projects? Consider the profitability of the work you're doing. Some clients are highly demanding of your time and effort, but don't bring in much income. Other clients are a delight to work with, recognize your skills, pay on time, and bring repeat business. Ideally, avoid the first kind, and find more of the second. Otherwise, mitigate the first kind with tight systems to keep their demands in check.

Most freelances make more money from doing larger projects where you can develop an effective working process with your client. Each new client means introductory research, "onboarding" and getting to know you, so if the job's a small one, it's often not very profitable. Look out for repeat work, or pursue sectors where you already have some expertise, so that you're not reinventing the wheel with each new client.

Cut costs

Luckily, copywriting is one of the lowest overhead businesses around, and you're unlikely to have substantial costs. But you may be tempted to splash out on office furniture, gadgets, stationery, and other perceived needs of a "real" business.

The only way to know the truth is to monitor costs. Review outgoings at least once a year. Some small regular outgoings can shock you. For example, I discovered that business travel and car parks were a big expense. I live in a rural area, and car miles are an expected part of doing business. But there are lots of other options now, such as Skype calls, email, and phone. I saved a huge amount by cutting down on meetings, and using the park-and-ride.

When you're freelance, saving time is a way of saving money. If you must have a meeting, set an agenda and keep it focused. Don't let phone meetings drift into general chat. Paint hard lines between what's business and what's personal.

Charge more

As you gain experience, consider putting up your rates. If you charge by the hour, clients will benefit from your speed and experience. This should come back to you in the form of higher rates for your services.

Also consider where you have a special expertise, and can add value. For example, could you charge more for content writing and uploading? Do you have sector knowledge which gives you special insights? Do you offer SEO and Analytics? Consider how you can package any additional skills as an extra service.

Get more sales

First, be honest about your available capacity. There's no point in marketing and getting in more work, if you can't turn it around quickly and efficiently. If you do have capacity, there are two ways to get more sales: find new clients, and upsell to existing clients.

Upselling to existing clients is easier than working with new ones. They already know you and are happy with your services, and you've developed a working process. You've already got through the intensive onboarding phase, and won't need to do nearly as much research.

So, first consider whether you can do more work for an existing client. For example, could you take over their blog and offer a regular monthly update, complete with images? Or an email newsletter? What about a suite of case studies to use as a marketing tool? Perhaps their brochure is looking a bit tired? Ask if they're considering a refresh. Often clients are aware of what they need to do, but just haven't got around to it. So your offer may come at exactly the right time.

Business growth

Once you've fully and realistically realized the potential of your own time, the only way to grow is to leverage the time of others. At some point, you may want to stop being a sole trader or freelance, and expand beyond the limitations of your own time. "Business growth" is a specific topic and strategy in business. It means high-value strategic expansion, rather than simply taking on extra support. If you're interested in knowing more about the strategic side, I strongly recommend *The E-Myth* by Michael Gerber, which brilliantly describes the usual pitfalls faced by small businesses.

To grow or not to grow?

For many creatives, the whole point of the freelance life is the freedom to choose and manage your own work. If you take on staff, you might find yourself back to being in an office, dealing with paperwork, and keeping others happy. You may end up in the situation you walked away from only a few years ago, except you're now the boss, and everyone depends on you. That's one reason to think carefully before taking on help.

But even with a well-established business, you can't rest on your laurels, and expect everything to run on smoothly until the end of your days. Evolution is built into the nature of business. There's even a school of thought that if you're not growing, you're actually failing. That's because businesses that don't grow and change can quickly be overtaken by those that do.

Equally, you can find yourself a victim of your own success, with so much work that the spinning plates start to wobble. If you become too busy, the new, available copywriter in town may suddenly take some of your work. So, a degree of steady evolution is inevitable and necessary. Taking on extra help is a natural extension of this.

155

Support services

Hiring a bookkeeper and accountant is the first step to experiencing the potential of growth. Delegating this to someone with far better skills gives you more time for your own productive work, and leads to fewer mistakes and headaches.

Another possibility is a virtual assistant. A VA can provide services including phone answering and secretarial, transcription and editing, as well as everyday online tasks such as updating blog posts, uploading photos, and social media, freeing you up to concentrate on your core work. It's possible to build towards a distributed company without ever needing premises, by bringing in other experts in this way.

Traditional expansion

If you're thinking of growing your business along more traditional lines, you'll probably need an office. This will mean extra overheads, including a dedicated phone line, internet, computer, services, and insurance. So, you need to be sure the extra work you can turn round will outweigh the extra cost by some distance.

In the creative industries, the time-honoured way to expand is to take on a junior or apprentice. Photographers and graphic designers often develop their businesses in this way. For copywriters, this is a less typical scenario, as anyone with the strong written communication skills you need is likely to be a highly capable graduate. With internships in high demand, you might consider taking on a bright graduate or English student, and training them in how to write for business.

A trainee will need a lot of your time at the start, so weigh up the extra productivity they can bring your business against the investment (time and money) needed to train them. Consider this as a long-term commitment, not a quick fix for your business.

One reason many sole traders don't take on a junior is that at some point, the trainee may think they can make more money doing the same work, without you as a middleman. Your newly skilled trainee might then take off, and start up on their own. So you need to keep developing your team, so that they're excited about the growth and future of your business, and encouraged to stay and be part of it.

Partner others

Partnering with another writer allows you to take up each other's slack, pitch for bigger jobs, cover holidays, and generally support each other. Alternatively, partner with complementary creative businesses, such as graphic designers, web designers and photographers. If you find these relationships fruitful, you may want to take the next step of forming a collective.

Over to You

That's all from me! I hope you've picked up some useful tips and processes on getting your own copywriting business launched, and are fired up with ideas.

Taking decisive action is vital for making a success of your business, so write down your next steps here, with deadlines, then get going!

Next Actions:

1. _____

2. _____

3. _____

4. Sign up for my newsletter @ www.method-writing.com

With very best wishes for your business writing success,

Jules

STARTER PROJECTS

These **Starter Projects** are for writers who have never done paid copywriting before. They will ease you in gently, and equip you with a bunch of portfolio pieces to show clients.

This section has four assignments designed to kickstart your portfolio. Do the assignments, and you'll end up with your own leaflet and a couple of good-looking samples to show. Flushed with this success, you can then start reaching out to paid clients, and building a work pipeline.

If you're a newbie, landing your first paid client is a huge deal. You're off the blocks, and have proven that you can make money. It's a great boost to your business confidence. And it's amazing how just that one piece of evidence can open doors.

But before you get there, you need to overcome the impasse of any new business: how can you get work without a track record? And how can you get a track record without evidence of work?

The answer is to do some "calling card" or "apprentice" pieces, to build your skills and confidence, and minimize the leap to your first paid gig. The suggested steps are:

1. Do a job for yourself as client. (Off the blocks)
2. Do a real job free for someone you know. (Listening skills)
3. Do a real job free for someone you don't know. (Stranger interview skills)
4. Turn this work into portfolio samples by partnering a graphic designer. (Networking skills)

Now, it's time to dive in at the deep end with **Assignment 1**.

Assignment 1: Your Own Flyer

Your first job is to write a leaflet for yourself. The aim is to experience both sides of the process, write a job, and let it go.

With your client hat on:
You're the client, and you need a business flyer for your copywriting business. For simplicity, go for a trifold A4 or DL size – a standard format often seen in leaflet holders. Now write down your requirements:

- What's the purpose of the leaflet?
- Who's the target market?
- What's the call to action? Do you want the reader to call, email, or visit a specific page on your website?
- What tone of voice is best for your target market?
- What's your USP?
- List 3 competitor websites or promos whose look you like.
- List any relevant colours, images and logos.
- Note your contact information.
- Note how long you expect this work to take, and how much you're prepared to pay.
- Add any other questions you have for the copywriter.

With your copywriter hat on:

- Read the brief and estimate how long the job should take.
- Start your timer.
- Write the leaflet.
- Put the copy in an email to yourself, and press "send."

Some questions:

- How long did both jobs take?
- Did the client's cost expectations match the time it took you?

162

- How helpful was the client's brief?
- What obstacles did you encounter?
- How would you do it differently next time?
- What else did you learn?

Notes and Tips

The chances are, this took longer than you thought. You were doing this for the first time, and it's not easy to write about and for yourself.

Did you come up against perfectionist tendencies? These are helpful for editing, less so for first-drafting. To keep this in check, write to the specific wordage needed for each job. Make a physical mockup to keep the focus tight, and collect good examples to compare yours with.

Keep a note of your process. Over time, you'll be able to hone this into a system for working more effectively.

Now move on to **Assignment 2**.

Assignment 2: Flyer For a Real Client

This is a free "calling card" project. The aim is to interview someone you know, in order to practise listening and responding to client needs.

- Find a friend with a small business who needs a new flyer. Let them know that this is a freebie.
- Use your notes from **Assignment 1**, create a briefing sheet for the client.
- Ask them to fill this in and email it to you.
- Follow this up with a 10' chat to clarify any missing information.
- Estimate how long the job will take.
- Write the leaflet. Note how long it really takes.
- Email the job to the client.

Optional: Call the client for feedback. Ask for their time estimate for this kind of job.

Once again, keep notes on what you've learned for future.

Notes and Tips

Clients may not be clear about they want, even when you give them a briefing sheet. Your questions may prompt them to think about surprisingly basic matters they haven't yet articulated, including even target market and competitors.

You and clients may have an unrealistic view of the time needed. You may both enjoy talking at length about the business, but need to keep a firm handle on research time.

Optional: if you know a graphic designer or design student who owes you a favour, get your words designed, to give the client a working leaflet, and you a portfolio piece. Or, go to www.moo.com and insert your copy into one of the templates. Moo allows you to send yourself and the client a free proof without paying. If the client likes the results, they may want to go ahead to print.

Now move on to **Assignment 3a or 3b:**

Assignment 3a: Speculative Sample

This is an unpaid, uncommissioned job for a real or imaginary client. In the creative industries, this is a common way to showcase your skills. If you know a designer in the same early-career boat as you, pair up. It could lead to a fruitful working relationship!

This time, write a larger, four-page leaflet in your preferred format. If you're working with a designer, be cautious about high-concept or unusual ideas. Small companies with small budgets often prefer not to risk out-there ideas. Companies with bigger marketing budgets may be more receptive.

To help with this assignment, use your notes from Assignment 1. You can also download a PDF on client interviews from my website (www.method-writing.com/downloads).

If you're in a hurry, cut to the chase, and do a real job for a real client.

Assignment 3b: Real Job, Real Client

A real freebie job for a real client hits several buttons at once. You'll practise the key skills of listening to the client, interpreting their brief, producing a couple of drafts, and responding to feedback. You'll hopefully also produce a piece of work which makes them happy, and does a good job of promoting their business.

Be honest with the client about your aims, and make clear this is an introductory freebie, or offer a special rate. This gives the client good value, and you a portfolio piece. Afterwards, if the client is happy, you can consider asking for a testimonial.

Assignment 4: Long Form Project

For this, write a Case Study. This is a "soft sell" informative piece that showcases an example of client work. Case studies have a substantial amount of copy, and provide a meatier example of your writing skills. They're particularly useful for business-to-business (B2B) and service companies. If you're a journalist, a case study will draw on skills you already know well: interviewing, reporting, and presenting complex topics in an accessible way.

If you like, use the same client you worked with for Assignment 3b.

Download the Case Study Template from www.method-writing. com/downloads.

Assignment 5: SEO Web Page

This project will give you a sense of the main concepts in search engine optimization (SEO). SEO can be highly technical, but understanding a few basics, such as keywords and meta descriptions, will greatly help your client work. SEO is constantly evolving in response to changing search engine algorithms, and some copywriters choose to specialize in it.

165

For this project, read the section on **SEO Copy**, and download the **SEO Web Page Template** from www.method-writing.com/downloads.

Assignment 6: Find a Design Collaborator

As soon as possible, get to know a professional graphic designer for ongoing collaboration – ideally a versatile one whose work you love. Graphic designers are a good source of work for freelance copywriters, and eventually, you should be able to return the favour. Find a skilled designer you get on well with, and you may have the makings of an excellent business team. Your words will look wonderful laid out in their beautiful, stylish designs, and their designs will stand out, thanks to your great copy.

If you can't find a likely graphic design professional near you, try a further education college that trains graphic design students. Students are often looking for real projects to work on, and your project may also benefit from their tutor's advice. This can be a chance to get your portfolio samples designed, and sow the seeds for future business collaboration.

Glossary

This glossary is a list of useful expressions used in business and marketing. A working knowledge of these will help you to connect with clients more effectively.

B2B
Business-to-business. B2B means selling to trade customers, rather than to general consumers. Copywriters sometimes specialize in either B2C (consumer-facing, retail etc) or B2B copywriting. As a jobbing copywriter, you're running a B2B business, since your market is other businesses. See also **B2C**.

B2C
Business-to-customer or business-to-consumer. See also **B2B**.

Bottom line
The final total in an account, after all costs are taken off.

Business development
Within a company or organisation, this usually refers to a senior sales and marketing role.

Client vs customer
Professional services (lawyers, accountants, hair stylists, copywriters) typically have clients. The retail and banking sectors have customers.

Hospitality and tourism have guests and visitors. Third sector organizations such as charities may have "users," service users," or "customers." Check with your clients to see what terminology they use.

Copywriter
The term "copywriter" is familiar to people in the creative sector, less so in other areas. Some copywriters call themselves "business writers" or "web content writers," depending on their specialism.

Corporate
"Corpus" is the Latin word for body, and a "corporate" company is one that can act as a single body, being constituted with a legal identity separate from its managers and owners (shareholders).

Development site
Also known as a "dev site" or "staging site." A site under development in a hidden corner of the internet, usually password-protected, and visible only to the web developer and client. When the project is complete, the site is published and "goes live."

Features and benefits
In marketing terminology, "features" are the attributes of a product or service, such as its size, shape, and function. "Benefits" are the results for the user: cures your cold, pulls in your stomach, and helps you to stay tidy. Equally important are "results" – the overriding motivation for buying a product: improves your appearance or health, or saves you time or money. These tap into our basic desires and fears: attracting a mate, improving our status, getting tasks done.

Marketing vs advertising
Marketing is an umbrella term covering advertising, public relations (PR), branding, market research, and several other disciplines. Most marketers specialize, rather than handling every discipline.

Micro-business

A business with fewer than 10 employees. This sector is an important "long tail" of economic activity. Most copywriters are micro-businesses.

Poster site

A basic website to establish a presence for a business, without extras such as online retail, a blog or a gallery. Typically, this kind of site has only a handful of pages, and is infrequently updated.

ROI

Return on investment. When spending on marketing, clients want to see benefits to their bottom line, usually expressed as percentage ROI. It can be hard to prove marketing ROI, as so many factors play a role in business success – the weather, fashion trends, luck, a new sales manager. But if you do have a good ROI statistic – eg your client reports that B&B bookings are up 60% since the new website – then use it.

SEO

Search engine optimization. An umbrella term for tactics to help sites improve their search engine rankings. SEO can be divided into "back end" technical tactics, "front end" design and user interface, and "content." See **SEO copy**.

SEO copy

See **SEO**. A writing form and style aimed at boosting a site's search engine rankings, usually incorporating key search words, URLs, meta descriptions, and Google Analytics data. SEO copy taken to an extreme is said to suffer from "keyword stuffing."

SME

Small or medium-sized enterprise. SMEs can range in size from ten employees to as many as 250.

Spinning

Copy changed by substituting synonyms, to give the appearance of new content. The aim is to fool search engines and plagiarism detectors, and achieve better site rankings without the expense of fresh copy. Search engines penalize this practice.

Supplier

The person or business that supplies goods or services. If you buy stationery, electricity, or support services for your own business, these companies are your suppliers. You supply your clients with copywriting services, so you're one of their suppliers.

Terms and conditions

T&Cs, "terms of use" or "terms of service" are a statement of how you conduct business. They may include sales and returns policies, payment terms, disclaimers, guarantees and other important contractual information.

Turnover

In the UK, business "turnover" means the same as "revenue" or "sales." High turnover doesn't necessarily mean a successful business. To work out profitability and sustainability, sales need to be balanced against the cost of running the business.

VAT

Value added tax, or GST (goods and services tax). Freelances with sales of under £83k in the UK don't need to register for VAT.

Further Reading

This list gets updated on my website, so check out this link for the latest recommendations: www.method-writing.com/downloads

Peter Bowerman (2009) *The Well-Fed Copywriter*

Michael Gerber (2009) *The E-Myth*

Roger Horberry (2009) *Brilliant Copywriting*

Andy Maslen (2009) *Write To Sell: The Ultimate Guide To Great Copywriting*

Andy Maslen (2010) *The Copywriting Sourcebook: How To Write Better Copy, Faster*

Andy Maslen (2010) *Write Copy, Make Money*

Andy Maslen (2015) *Persuasive Copywriting: Using Psychology to Engage, Influence and Sell*

Index

About Jules Horne

I'm an award-winning writer and university teacher from Scotland, where I live with my partner on the edge of the Cheviot Hills. As well as running my copywriting business, Texthouse, I teach on the MA in Creative Writing with the Open University, where I helped to write the Script strand. Like most copywriters, I've been passionate about words all my life, which led me into BBC journalism and German government translation, via a German and French degree from Oxford University. I wrote this book for the many creative writers and writing students who want to make a living from their skills.

If you've found this book helpful, visit www.method-writing.com and **sign up for my mailing list** to receive tips and templates for your copywriting business. And I'd love it if you could review this book with a short comment on Amazon – it really helps! To get in touch with me directly, email info@method-writing.com.

www.method-writing.com

Other Books by Jules Horne

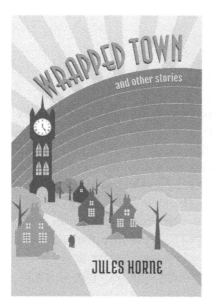 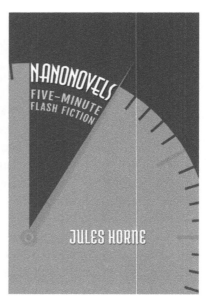

WRAPPED TOWN

"Magical and profound".

Dolly the sheep is anointed by angels, an old horse bequeaths its bones... 22 stories of extraordinary imagination with a touch of Scottish Gothic.

ISBN: 978-0-9934354-3-0

Available at:
myBook.to/wrappedtown

NANONOVELS

150 days. 150 stories.

What happens when library, laptop, and scentific method collide? An exuberant fiction debut from an award-winning Scottish writer.

ISBN: 978-0-9934354-1-6

Available at:
myBook.to/nanonovels